CONTENTS

Unit 19

The Aftermath of World War I

Prepared by Arthur Marwick for the Course Team

CONTENTS AND OBJECTIVES

Preliminaries

This is a relatively short unit, designed to serve as a link between the detailed study of World War I which you have just completed, and the detailed study of World War II which follows. Above all it is intended as a prelude to Dr Adamthwaite's study of the causes of World War II, and to your own study of A. J. P. Taylor's *The Origins of the Second World War*,[1] which is the essential text for this and next week. You should have plenty of time, too, to do a really thorough study of the Treaty of Versailles which is printed in your documents unit—Unit 18 E1.

Your *essential* reading for Sections 19.1 and 19.2 of this unit is Roberts, *Europe 1880–1945*,[2] Chapter 10, Chapters 2 and 3 of Taylor, and the selections from the Treaty of Versailles printed in your documents unit as document E1. For Section 19.3 the prescribed reading is Chapter 11 of Roberts, and the article which forms an appendix to Unit 16, W. E. Leuchtenburg, 'The New Deal and the Analogue of War'.

You are already familiar enough with Roberts to appreciate it as a first-class general textbook. But A. J. P. Taylor's *The Origins of the Second World War* perhaps needs a few words of introduction. Although in this unit we are only looking in detail at Chapters 2 and 3, it would obviously be good sense to start the book from the beginning. The new foreword, entitled, 'Second Thoughts' is a very good introduction to Taylor's approach to history. We shall be looking at this question again in the next unit when we discuss the origins of the Second World War in some detail, and have a radio programme in which Taylor is a participant. Here I should just like to direct your attention to one or two key thoughts in this foreword (you might, if you feel so inclined, refresh your memory as to what I say about A. J. P. Taylor in the first-year textbook *The Nature of History*,[3] pp. 187–93 and 235–8). First of all note his continual harping on the theme that events tend to happen by accident, rather than due to the conscious planning of statesmen; for example, at the foot of page 10, he says of Hitler that 'he exploited events far more than he followed precise coherent plans'. Note Taylor's reference to Maitland, one of the greatest of all professional historians (again you might consult *The Nature of History* here). Taylor is very much in this professional tradition when on page 26 he says: 'it is not part of a historian's duty to say what ought to have been done. His sole duty is to find out what was done and why.' The detached attitude, and perhaps even an element of cynicism, can be seen in the remark on page 9: 'As a historian, I recognize Powers will be Powers.' Incidentally, this too is an excellent example of the wit which makes Taylor such a pleasure to read. On the other hand, you may feel that certain prejudices on his part are betrayed by his very final sentence in the foreword: 'In international affairs there was nothing wrong with Hitler except that he was a German.'

Chapter 1 concerns the origins of the Second World War, our topic for the next unit, and, in fact, it establishes a very neat link between Units 14 and 20. Once you have finished Chapter 3, I think you will find it best to proceed to work on this correspondence material. When you have done that, you can pick up again at Chapter 4 and complete the book in preparation for next week's correspondence material.

---

[1] A. J. P. Taylor, *The Origins of the Second World War*, Penguin Books (SET BOOK).

[2] J. M. Roberts, *Europe 1880–1945*, Longman (SET BOOK).

[3] A. Marwick, *The Nature of History*, Macmillan, 1971 (A100 SET BOOK).

19.1 THE PEACE TREATIES AND THE COVENANT OF THE LEAGUE OF NATIONS

19.1.1 The general problems of peacemaking

Before proceeding any further with this unit, be sure you have read Chapter 10 of Roberts and Chapters 2 and 3 of Taylor, preferably in that order. (You may, if you seek guidance in your reading, glance ahead to the questions which follow.) You will find it helpful to note down the main points each author makes as you read.

Exercise 1

After you have done this reading note down answers to the following questions.

1   This is a purely factual question, but I think it is important for you to get the answer to it clear in your mind. The Treaty of Versailles was only one part of the entire peace settlement at the end of the war. What were the other treaties, and with which countries were they signed? Also note against each treaty the main problems with which it dealt.

2   In a striking sentence, A. J. P. Taylor passes judgement on the moral validity of the Treaty of Versailles. There is a rather noticeable echo of this sentence in Roberts (note that the Taylor book was first published in 1961, whereas Roberts was first published in 1967). Try to identify the two sentences.

3   On the question of American withdrawal from European affairs, Roberts has very clear views. What are these views? What views does A. J. P. Taylor have on this issue? Which interpretation do you find more persuasive?

4   Throughout Chapters 2 and 3 Taylor consistently develops a basic point in regard to what happened in the military sphere in October and early November 1918, and he sees here a fundamental flaw in the whole structure of the peace settlement. What is this point?

Specimen Answer

1   Treaty of St Germain with Austria. Main problems concern Italian territories formerly governed by Austria, and non-Italian territories coveted by Italy belonging to Austria, and the whole question of the 'succession States', the States formed by the various national groups within the former Austrian empire (remember their claims had been one of the causes of tension in the years before 1914).

Treaty of Neuilly with Bulgaria. Bulgaria to lose territory to her neighbours, the Dobrudja to Rumania, Western Thrace and Bulgaria's strip of the Aegean coast to Greece. Bulgaria also to pay reparations to the allies.

Treaty of Sèvres, replaced by Treaty of Lausanne, with Turkey. Main problems the collapse of the Turkish empire, with the ensuing claims of her Arab former subjects, and the rivalry between the new Nationalist Turkey and Greece.

Treaty of Trianon with Hungary. Main question the allocation of former Hungarian territory, including three-quarters of Hungary's former inhabitants, to Czechoslovakia, Rumania and Yugoslavia. The situation was complicated by the brief seizure of power by the Bolshevik Bela Kun.

2   The Taylor sentence is: 'The Peace of Versailles lacked moral validity from the start.' This is echoed by Roberts when he writes: 'Shortcomings such as these meant that a moral cloud hung over the Versailles settlement from the start.'

3   Roberts says (p. 315): 'The American Government, above all, fatally weakened the Treaty by failing to secure its ratification by Congress and by abandoning the Anglo-American Guarantee to France.' He repeats this view on page 332, when he says: 'The results of this withdrawal of the United States from an organization which might have transformed European affairs are incalculable.'

A. J. P. Taylor does not regard the American withdrawal as being so serious for the peace of Europe as does Roberts. Speaking of the withdrawal, he says at the top of page 56: 'Though this was a blow against the new order, it was not such a decisive blow as was later made out.' Taylor argues that what was really crucial was the weakness and disagreement among the European powers themselves, and that, anyway, America continued to interfere as much, and as little, in European affairs as seemed to her necessary; he argues that the actual detail of whether she accepted the Versailles settlement and the League Covenant was not really particularly relevant. I find this persuasive. Putting the blame on American withdrawal does rather seem to be finding an excuse for European failures. The actual detail of formal American adherence would certainly not have made any difference without considerable changes in overall American attitudes and policies.

4   Taylor's basic point is that at the end of the war the allies did not conquer and dismember Germany, but rather concluded an armistice with what was substantially an intact Germany. He sees the continued existence of an intact Germany as continuing 'the German problem' as a potential cause of a future war.

Exercise 2

1   We saw in Question 2 of the previous exercise that both Roberts and Taylor refer to the moral quality of the Treaty of Versailles and to its shortcomings. They both agree that one feature, in particular, was especially disastrous from the point of view of the preservation of future peace. What is this?

2   It might be argued that the basic Taylor point revealed in Question 4 in the previous exercise is both unduly cynical and strongly anti-German. What comments on it might (a) a less anti-German historian, and (b) a pacifist historian, make on it?

Specimen Answers

1   Reparations

2   A less anti-German historian might argue that the so-called 'German problem' needn't be a problem at all, and certainly need not threaten war. A pacifist historian might comment that what Taylor is really saying is that wars solve nothing.

19.1.2   The Covenant of the League of Nations

I hope that from your reading in the two prescribed books you will have grasped the essential nature and scope of the problems which faced the peacemakers in 1919. A war on such unprecedented scale obviously left problems of an unprecedented nature. Insulated as we have been in these islands, we can easily forget the immense problems involved in the collapse of old political frontiers, from the mixing of races in particular areas, from the reallocation of territorial boundaries, and from the transfer of populations (though recent events in Northern Ireland may give us a few hints).

The Treaty of Versailles altogether consists of 440 articles and it takes up 230 pages of Volume LIII of the *Parliamentary Papers* for 1919. In Document E1 of your documents collection (Unit 18) I print substantial selections from the Treaty. In order to give you an idea of the scale of the Treaty and the ground covered by it, I have indicated the nature and size of the most important omissions.

Now I want you to read Part I of the Treaty, The Covenant of the League of Nations.

Exercise 1

1   What evidence is there in the Covenant itself that the League was, as many Germans and many left-wingers in Britain maintained, merely 'a League of Victorious Powers'?

2   It was often said in the 'twenties and 'thirties, and afterwards, that a fundamental weakness of the League of Nations was that it 'lacked teeth'. That is to say, it was not prepared to threaten potential and actual aggressors with military force. What clauses in the Covenant contradict this contention?

3   (a)   What proposals in regard to Germany's former colonial possessions are incorporated into the Covenant?

   (b)   What attitudes towards the peoples of colonial dependencies are revealed in the Covenant?

Specimen Answers and Discussion

1   Clause 1 of Article 4 says that the Council of the League is to consist of the representatives of the principal Allied and Associated Powers, with representatives of four other members of the League. It could be argued that this shows the victorious powers establishing their position in the Council, which as the following clauses make clear is the more important of the two chambers (Council and Assembly) of the League.

2   *Article 10* says that in the case of aggression or the threat or danger of aggression, the Council shall advise upon how this is to be met: military action is not excluded. Clause 2 of *Article 16* states that if any member of the League does resort to war in disregard of *Articles 12, 13 or 15*, the Council shall recommend to the several governments concerned what effective military, naval and air force the members of the League should contribute. Clause 3 makes it clear that members of the League will be expected to permit the passage through their territories of the armed forces of other members of the League. This article in total clearly envisages the possibility of military action by the League in order to deter aggression. [John Ferguson points out that the requirement of unanimity on the part of the Council effectively negated all of these provisions. But, in my view, this does not invalidate my point that the teeth were there; *if only the Powers were prepared to put them to work.*]

3   (a)   The key clause is clause 2 of *Article 22* which makes it clear that the colonies are to be divided up amongst the leading members of the League, who are supposed to administer these colonies as 'mandates' on behalf of the League.

   (b)   'Patronizing' is the word that springs most readily to my mind.

19.1.3   The Treaty of Versailles

Now read the remainder of the Treaty of Versailles. In order to fix the main shape and content in your mind, note down the titles of each part, and underneath them briefly summarize the content of the part.

This is one for you to do without any further help from me!

As a document, the Versailles Treaty in itself tells us many things. Clearly it is the most authoritative source for the way in which the map of Europe was redrawn (the Treaty itself, of course, contains many detailed maps, necessarily omitted in your documents collection—but see the map on page 15) at the end of the war, the way in which Germany was treated, and all the immediate attendant implications of this. But we will always have to balance what is actually stated as an intention in the document against what, in the light of subsequent events, we know actually happened. We will have to watch out for clauses which may be largely designed for their propaganda value, either in expressing high motives, or, perhaps even in expressing undue hostility towards Germany. (Remember the bitter feelings towards Germany in the Allied countries.) From the document itself we can see the very real complexities and difficulties which faced the peacemakers. From the detail in some parts of the Treaty you can see what peacemaking is really like, as distinct from brief text-book accounts which merely summarize the broad principles; you can see what is involved in putting certain broad decisions into practice. The Treaty of Versailles expresses definite intentions about settling the map of Europe. But, as with all historical documents it contains an element of 'unwitting testimony'. That is to say we do learn things from it about the fundamental assumptions of the men who drafted it, and even little incidental bits of information about social and political conditions in Europe.

Figure 1   Clemenceau, 1841–1929 (Mansell Collection).

Figure 2   Woodrow Wilson, 1856–1924 (Mansell Collection).

On the whole, I want you to do most of the work for yourself, checking each clause as you read it against any comments made on it by Roberts and Taylor. However, I want to list here some of the problems which are either not dealt with by Taylor and Roberts or which, in my view, are not sufficiently emphasized. Keep them in mind as you read the Treaty.

1   The human and administrative problems involved in redrawing frontiers (particularly where nationalities are mixed) and in transfers of population.

2   Attempts to maintain the effects of Germany's military defeat by reductions in her military, political and economic potential.

3   The issues which in the years to come were to be major sources of tension between Germany and the other powers (you will need the help of Taylor and Roberts in identifying these).

4   The different arguments and the different vested interests of the various Allied statesmen (and nations) which lie behind different clauses (Roberts and Taylor are useful, though in a very general way—all that is needed here).

Exercise 1

Now make notes against each of these four headings.

Exercise 2

1   With regard to what actually happened in the 1920s, comment on *Article 160*.

2   Comment on the three-line preamble to Part V, together with clause 1 of *Article 8*

  (a)   from the point of view of the real intentions of the drafters of the Treaty;
  (b)   with regard to what actually happened in the 1920s, and German reactions to this.

3   Throughout the entire Treaty there is a good deal of 'unwitting testimony' as to immediate political events, social conditions and social attitudes. Comment on

Figure 3   Vittorio Orlando, 1860–1952, Italian Prime Minister, 1917–19 and leader of the Italian delegation to the Paris Peace Conference 1919–20 (Staatsbibliothek Berlin. Preussicher Kulturbesitz Bildarchiv).

any points you think relevant here, making particular reference to what has already been said about the effects of war in bringing about social change (disruption, test, military participation, psychological effects, and all that).

4   Roberts (p. 316) speaks of 'the Conference's general neglect of economic issues'. Having read the Treaty yourself, do you agree with this?

Specimen Answers

Exercise 1

1   In connection with the allocation of Eupen and Malmedy to Belgium, registers are to be opened to allow inhabitants to record their desire to remain under German sovereignty. A special Commission is to settle the exact frontier, 'taking into account the economic factors and means of communication'. Former German nationals will become Belgian, save that those who became resident after August 1 1914 will require a permit from the Belgian Government; however, former German nationals can opt for German nationality, in which case they must move to Germany, freely taking their movables with them, and retaining their rights in their immovable property. The German Government is to hand over all documents, registers, etc., to the Belgian Government (this is a very vital point, given the complexities of modern government and is repeated in regard to every transfer of territory). Special provisions will have to be made in regard to the public debt of the transferred territories (*Article 39*).

The final decision in regard to sovereignty over the Saar is to be left to a plebiscite held in fifteen years' time.

In Alsace-Lorraine problems consequent upon the return of these territories to France shall be subject to separate agreements between France and Germany; it is envisaged that some inhabitants may retain German nationality.

It is in the area of Germany's frontiers with the reconstituted Polish State that the problems are most complex. The details of the plebiscite to be held in Upper Silesia are spelled out, together with the provisions for temporary administration by an Allied Commission. There are the necessary provisions for opting between Polish and German nationality and for place of residence, and there is special provision to guard the right of political (i.e. nationalist) protest (*Article 88*). Most important of all is *Article 93*, designed to safeguard German minority rights in Poland. Such safeguards recur throughout the Treaty, but obviously the problems associated with racial, linguistic and religious minorities could not all be solved by the clauses of the Treaty alone. The settlement of Germany's boundaries in the east created a 'Polish corridor' separating East Prussia from the rest of Germany (see Map 1). *Article 89* guarantees free communication between the two parts of Germany. The issue of nationality comes up again in regard to Memel (Section X); and the setting up of the Free City of Danzig also creates special problems. Danzig was in fact predominantly German, so note the provision against 'any discrimination . . . to the detriment of citizens of Poland and other persons of Polish origin or speech' (*Article 104* (5)).

2   The main boundary changes of Part III scarcely amount to such an attempt, but Section III, providing for the demilitarization of the left bank of the Rhine could certainly be so interpreted. More relevant is Germany's renouncement of her overseas possessions in Part IV. And most important of all are the military, naval and air clauses of Part V, and the Reparations clauses of Part VIII. The Guarantee clauses (Part XIV), particularly in regard to the institution of allied occupation forces, would also seem, at least for the time they are intended to last, to be designed to maintain the effects of Germany's defeat.

Figure 4 (opposite)   Map showing territorial adjustments of Treaty of Versailles (based on a map in A. J. P. Taylor, Origins of the Second World War, Penguin Books, 1963, p. 338).

14

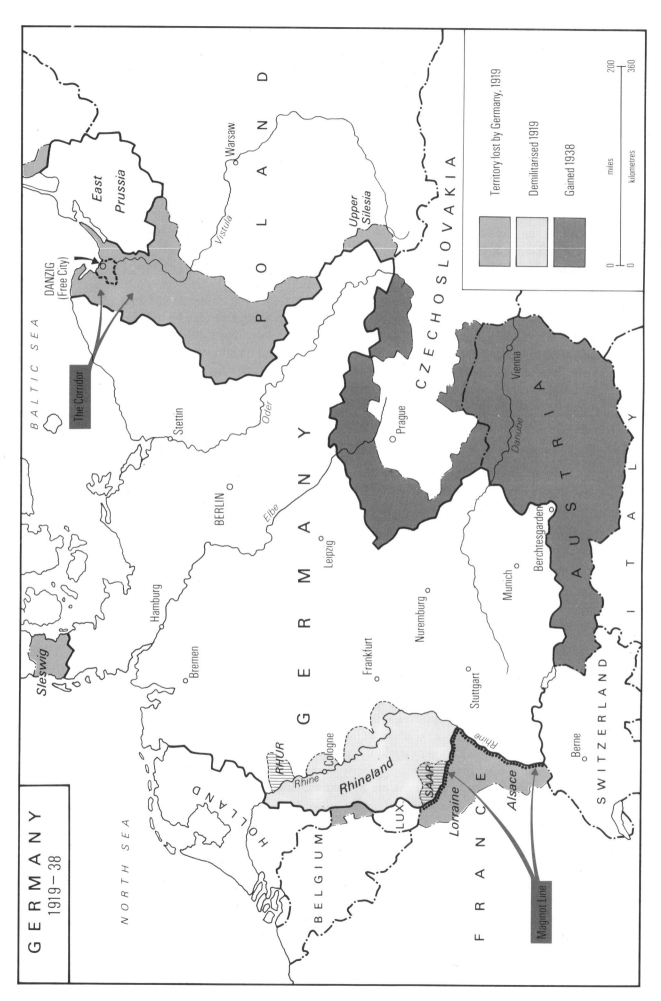

GERMANY
1919–38

Territory lost by Germany, 1919
Demilitarised 1919
Gained 1938

miles   200
0
kilometres 360
0

BALTIC SEA

NORTH SEA

DANZIG
(Free City)

East
Prussia

The Corridor

POLAND

Warsaw

Vistula

Upper
Silesia

Sleswig

Stettin

Oder

CZECHOSLOVAKIA

Hamburg

BERLIN

Elbe

Leipzig

Prague

Vienna

Danube

AUSTRIA

Bremen

GERMANY

Frankfurt

Nuremburg

Munich

Berchtesgaden

ITALY

HOLLAND

RUHR

Cologne

Rhine

Rhineland

Stuttgart

SAAR

Rhine

Berne

BELGIUM

LUX

Lorraine

Alsace

SWITZERLAND

Maginot Line

F R A N C E

15

3   The main issues are the complicated arrangements made in regard to the Saar, and the eventual provision for a plebiscite; the embargo on any amalgamation between Austria and Germany; the setting up of Czechoslovakia, including a German-speaking minority; the establishment of the Polish corridor and the Free City of Danzig (as Roberts and Taylor both stress, German statesmen, even at Locarno, felt unable to accept the permanence of her Eastern frontiers). Reparations, the military clauses, and the demilitarization of the Rhineland, were also, of course, continuing sources of tension.

4   Obviously, if you had the sources, you could write volumes on this. On the basis of your reading in Roberts and Taylor, all I expect you to note here is that the League of Nations clauses, and the nationality clauses, were very much influenced by the ideas of President Wilson, that the harsher clauses were very much at the insistence of Clemenceau; and that Lloyd George actually got the provisions in regard to Danzig altered in Germany's favour (a 'Free City' instead of a Polish one as Wilson and Clemenceau originally intended). The Reparations clauses and that calling for the trial of the Kaiser (*Article 227*) were in part occasioned by popular anti-German hysteria in Britain and France. [It should further be noted, as Dr Adamthwaite points out, that all the peacemakers were much influenced by their fear of Bolshevism.[1] Although many people at the time, including the Germans, considered the treaty harsh, it might have been harsher still but for the apprehension of Bolshevism. The fear was that if Germany were not treated with some moderation she would be driven further into revolution and into the arms of Russia.]

Exercise 2

1   Germany managed in part to evade this article by carrying out military training and manoeuvres on Russian territory.

2   (a)   A. J. P. Taylor argues that it was never the real intention of the Allies to carry through reductions in armaments to the extent implied in these two parts of the treaty.

    (b)   The allies certainly never did reduce armaments on the scale implied by the treaty; this gave the Germans yet another grievance and, of course, helped to provoke the arrangements with Russia mentioned in the answer to Question 1 above.

3   With regard to immediate political events, we learn from clause 1 of the annex to *Article 88* of the existence of Workmen's and Soldiers' Councils in Poland early in 1919. Part XIII (Labour) brings out very clearly the social change aspect of the war, and could be attributed to the military participation effect, in combination, perhaps, with the psychological effects of war. Much the same comment could be made on *Article 23* of the League Covenant, and, indeed, the idealistic aspects of the League Covenant could in part be attributed again to the psychological effects of war. It is particularly noteworthy that wherever plebiscites are to be held, women, equally with men, are to have the vote. On the other hand, note that wherever it is a question of choosing nationality, wives are bound by the decisions of their husbands.

4   I have indicated the amount of space taken up by the economic clauses of the Treaty, although I have omitted many of them because they are so detailed and technical. Because of these omissions it may be hard for you to give a balanced answer to this question. But, in my view, if we pay attention to the actual proportions of the Treaty devoted to economic matters, and of course these spill over

[1] Roberts and Taylor have nothing on this. See, if you are interested, Arno J. Mayer, *Politics and the Diplomacy of Peacemaking: Containment and Counterrevolution at Versailles, 1918–1919*, Weidenfeld and Nicolson, 1968.

into very many other sections of the Treaty, I don't myself think it is fair to speak of a 'general neglect of economic issues'. The economic dispositions may have been unwise; but that is another matter.

Figure 5   Lloyd George, 1863–1945 (Mansell Collection).

Figure 6   Ramsay MacDonald, 1886–1937 (Mansell Collection).

Exercise 3

One of the four major themes in this *War and Society* Course concerns 'attempts to control or abolish wars'. What parts of the entire Treaty of Versailles could be regarded as intended to fulfil these objectives, and how far did they prove effective?

Specimen Answers

Section I (Covenant of the League of Nations). You must come to your own decisions about the effectiveness of the League of Nations—I've already given you some hints of my own views.

Although I have suggested a rather dubious motivation behind *Article 227* (bringing the Kaiser to trial), this, together with *Article 228*, can be seen as enshrining the principle that civilized nations will take action against war crimes. Neither article (as Taylor informs you) was put into practice, but the principle was to be raised again at the end of World War II.

The attempts in the Treaty to express the rights of nationality were also partly intended to avert future potential causes of war. If they were not wholly successful this was perhaps more due to the complexities of the problems than to major defects in the Treaty (with regard to the German-speaking minority in Czechoslovakia: this was a case where full expression to nationality was *not* granted). Note what Roberts says on this issue in the three paragraphs beginning on the middle of page 312, and President Wilson's dismayed exclamation, which he quotes on page 313.

To the extent that, in practice, they were one-sided (and perhaps even hypocritical) the general disarmament clauses of the Treaty were scarcely effective. Nor, since they were eventually evaded, were the German military and disarmament clauses effective.

19.2   THE INTERNATIONAL SITUATION IN THE 1920s

As we saw from Unit 14, it is sometimes said that the German threat to the balance of power in Europe was a major cause of the First World War. Both Roberts (Chapter 10) and Taylor (Chapters 2 and 3) are very clear about the nature of the European power balance at the end of the First World War.

Exercise 1

What do they regard as the state of the European balance at the end of the First World War?

Specimen Answer

Both Roberts and Taylor stress that the effect of the war was potentially to leave Germany even stronger as against the other European powers than she had been in 1914, particularly because of the collapse of Austria-Hungary and, for the time being, of Russia. In one sense this is a development of Taylor's point about the Allied failure to proceed to a total conquest of Germany.

As Roberts puts it at the bottom of page 305: 'Germany might be prostrate, but her potential was intact; there had been no complete overthrow of Germany ending with a great occupation by the victorious armies.' Again, at the foot of page 313 Roberts says:

Germany, although prostrate in 1918, was potentially a great power, and the only one in central Europe. She was now surrounded by weak states with German *irredenta* whose claims would no longer be ignored in Berlin, as those before 1914 had been in order to preserve Austria-Hungary.

Pay particular attention to what Taylor says in the last paragraph of page 43 running over to the first half of page 44, and culminating in this statement:

The constellation of Europe was profoundly changed—and to Germany's advantage. Where there had formerly been a Great Power on her eastern frontier, there was now a No-Man's land of small states and beyond it an obscurity of ignorance. No one could tell for long years after 1918, whether Russia had any power and, if so, what use she would make of it.

Note, too, what Taylor says on the lower half of page 48 about the potential economic preponderance of Germany over France. Again, in a theme which we meet over and over again, he concludes:

More than this, the old balance of power, which formerly did something to restrain Germany, had broken down. Russia had withdrawn; Austria-Hungary had vanished. Only France and Italy remained, both inferior in manpower—and still more in economic resources, both exhausted by the war.

In the whole discussion of the origins of the Second World War, this question of the complete disruption of the balance of power is one to which historians now give a good deal of attention. The Cambridge historian, F. H. Hinsley, has particularly stressed what he sees as the peculiar 'international instability' of the period after 1918 as one of the determining causes of the Second World War.[1] [However, compare all this with what Dr Adamthwaite, who feels that Taylor overstates his case, says in the next unit.]

The particular problem of France has received much attention. The terrible bleeding of the war, which aggravated the continuing decline in her population increase, the devastation caused to her north-eastern areas, and the dreadful consequences which attended upon the faith of her generals in taking the offensive at all costs, created a deep reluctance among politicians and people to contemplate anything but a defensive war in the future, though for the time being this reluctance was obscured by Clemenceau's militance at Versailles and after, and by France's ever active search for international alliances.

Historians of British foreign policy, too, have recently pointed out more and more that Britain's position after the First World War was considerably weaker than it seemed. Direct participation by the United States and by Japan in world affairs, as seen in their part in the war, had brought an enormous visible accession of power to these nations; accordingly the relative power of the British Empire was in fact diminished. In the dire necessities of war Britain had been happy to see Japan and the United States build up their respective naval strengths, but, again, at the end of the war, this meant that Britain was no longer the world's supreme naval power. This fact was recognized at the Washington Naval Conference held during the winter of 1921–2. The naval ratios agreed upon there were: United States and Britain as 5, to Japan's 3, to 1·6 for France and Italy. At the London conference of 1930 the American and British ratio to Japan was amended slightly in favour of the latter, to 10:7 (France and Italy refused to accept the decisions of this conference). The old two-power standard of pre-1914 days (that is to say, the principle that Britain's navy should be as strong as the next two most powerful navies in the world combined) had gone for good. Britain's position as an impregnable island fortress was further weakened by the new potential of air power revealed and strengthened by the war. It was true that British statesmen in the inter-war years were to show a tendency to exaggerate the threat of air attack, but as long as this fear existed, it had a definite influence on British foreign policy.

Participation in the war effort strengthened the position of the British Dominions, which in various ways were able to establish a real independence in the early 1920s. Again this served as a limitation on the power and resources which Britain could automatically bring to bear in questions of war and peace.[2]

Now let's be sure that we have the main outlines of the changing European situation in the 'twenties firmly in mind. One could use various possible themes to organize the material, but we might as well settle for the three suggested by Roberts on page 325:

1   The existence of revisionism.

2   The growth of the new League of Nations and the hopes it aroused.

3   The constant pursuit of security by France.

These themes are dealt with clearly and systematically by Roberts, and scarcely need much further elaboration here. In following through your reading on European international history in the 1920s, you should also pay special attention to

---

[1] See especially Chapters 12–15 of F. H. Hinsley, *Power and the Pursuit of Peace: Theory and Practice in the History of Relations between States*, Cambridge University Press, 1967. The entire book, which is available in paperback, makes for stimulating supplementary reading to many of the topics of this whole *War and Society* course.

[2] The best account of British foreign policy which places proper emphasis on these points is F. S. Northedge, *The Troubled Giant*, Praeger, 1967; an excellent shorter account, is W. N. Medlicott, *British Foreign Policy since Versailles, 1919–1963*, Methuen, University Paperback, 1968.

4   the major developments in the Reparations issue and in the issue generally of Germany's relationships with the other Western powers, and

5   the position of Russia, and the attitudes of the other powers towards her. Finally, a point which is often neglected (Taylor deals with it but Roberts scarcely touches on it)

6   the question of the military preparedness and policies of the main Western countries.

Now, for your own interest, note down the main points in regard to the first two of Roberts's themes. In particular, you might briefly draw up a kind of balance sheet of achievements and failings of the League of Nations.

Exercise 2

Question 1

With regard to the third theme (the French quest for security), note down here the basic feature of the alliance system which France devised in the 1920s.

Specimen Answer

The Cordon Sanitaire of alliances with the new East European countries. (Be sure that you know from your prescribed books exactly what these alliances were.) [Dr Adamthwaite again points out here that it has been argued that these alliances were also intended as barriers against Bolshevism.]

Question 2

With regard to this general French policy, A. J. P. Taylor, in the middle of page 64, offers one of his many shining aphorisms: 'The Anglo-French Entente and the Eastern Alliances did not supplement each other; they cancelled out.' Explain this.

Question 3

Note the main features of the history of Reparations and of Germany's relationships with the Western powers.

Question 4

What main points can be made about the military policies of Britain and France in the 1920s?

Question 5

What are the main features of Russia's relationships with the other powers in the 1920s?

Specimen Answers

Question 2

Taylor does develop the point in the sentences following his aphorism; rather the same point is made by Roberts in the middle paragraph on page 340. However, rather than just repeat what is said in your textbooks, I want to be sure that you are absolutely clear about the implications of this point. The point is that, although France hoped that her eastern alliances would serve to protect herself, they could only have any reality if France was prepared to honour her obligations to go to the defence of her eastern allies if they were threatened by Germany. But France alone scarcely now had the power to defend these eastern powers. If she took action in the west in the form of invading Germany, she would not have the support of Britain. Britain would only be likely to give support to France if France herself were invaded; in such an eventuality there would in any case be no help available for the eastern Countries.

Taylor refers to this situation as a 'deadlock'. Perhaps it need not have been so if Britain had shown more understanding of the importance of the East European countries, and more willingness to take an interest in their affairs. But if you know anything of subsequent European history, you can perhaps see in this so-called 'deadlock', the basis of the Munich crisis.

Question 3

The first Reparations crisis came when Germany defaulted on payments to France in December 1922. This led to the French occupation of the Ruhr, which in itself produced no advantages for France. The Dawes plan of 1924 for the first time settled a maximum annual figure for Germany's obligation. The Young plan of 1930 fixed the total amount.

Germany was practically brought into full co-operation with the other European powers in the Treaty of Locarno of December 1925. This was a treaty of guarantee which bound Britain, France, Germany, Belgium and Italy, to uphold the territorial *status quo*. Britain and Italy were guarantors of the convention signed by the other three powers and would be obliged to take action in the event of a flagrant breach of the agreement.

Perhaps even more important, Germany now joined the League of Nations.

Question 4

There was no total disarmament in Britain, but the mass army of the Great War was immediately disbanded, and there was little effort to build up armoured forces. The 'ten year principle' was fundamental to British military policy up to 1932: that is to say the heads of the fighting services were instructed that they need not anticipate a major war for at least ten years.

France did not disarm either, but neither did she attempt to build up the kind of military potential which would have been necessary to make her *Cordon Sanitaire* policy a reality. Increasingly, France thought defensively. Military service was reduced to one year in 1928; and in 1930 France began to build her great strategic defensive line, the Maginot line.

Question 5

Perhaps one of the most significant single features in the history of Russian relations with the rest of the world since the revolution, is the fact of Western intervention in the Russian Civil War. Intervention had actually begun during the World War as an attempt to bolster those elements in Russia still prepared to fight on against Germany, but as it continued after the end of the war it more and more assumed a deliberate anti-Bolshevik character.[1] In 1922 Russia and Germany, still the two European outcasts, concluded a Treaty at Rapallo. In 1924 the British Labour Government granted *de jure* recognition to the Russian Bolshevik Government. By the end of the 1920s Russia was again receiving loans from the West, and it was quite clear that there was no real threat of Russian attempts to spread communism by military means; none the less Russia remained very much an outsider in the European scene.

[1] If you want to read further in this topic (not part of your syllabus) see R. H. Ullman, *Intervention and the War*, Vol. 1 of *Anglo Soviet Relations 1917–21*, Princeton University Press: Oxford University Press, 1961, and John Silverlight, *The Victor's Dilemma: Allied Intervention in the Russian Civil War*, Barrie and Jenkins, 1970.

Figure 7   Aristide Briand, 1862–1932 (Mansell Collection).

Figure 8   Gustav Stresemann, 1878–1929 (Staatsbibliothek Berlin. Preussicher Kulturbesitz Bildarchiv).

Figure 9   Wall Street, 24 October 1929 (Associated Press).

Exercise 3

Now, bearing these various themes in mind, draw up a balance sheet for the end of the '20s showing the prospects for continuing peace.

Specimen Answer

Obviously this is very much a matter of individual interpretation, and perhaps even speculation. Here, briefly, are my own thoughts.

As Germany recovered, the 'international instability', or distorted balance of power, grew all the more serious. However, it might be reasonable to assume that a contented Germany would not be a threat to peace; the problem then was to ensure that now that Germany was getting stronger, she did not still have serious grievances. Germany had been brought into the League of Nations, and seemed in the Locarno Agreements and Kellogg-Briand pact (see *Roberts*, p. 341) to be willing to play a peaceful part in international relations. Reparations, as a real financial issue, were practically settled. Indeed, Germany had received far more in loans than she ever paid in Reparations; none the less, the issue was one which continued to rankle in Germany. While it was still not clear that the League of Nations could or would be effective in disputes between major powers, none the less the organization had survived, had shown itself effective in many minor ways, and was now

Figure 10 James N. Rosenberg, October 29 Dies Irae (Philadelphia Museum of Art, Carl Zigrasser Collection).

more genuinely a League of Nations than it had been in 1919. Ramsay Macdonald, when British prime minister, had attempted to give the League real prestige.

In the aftermath of the Locarno treaties, France at last seemed to believe that she had received genuine guarantees of security.

None of the possible revisionist claims seemed in themselves likely to provoke a major war; but there remained potential trouble-spots in regard to Germany's frontiers with Poland, with Czechoslovakia, and in regard to her relationship with Austria.

Italy (remember Unit 2 and Allport's arguments on 'expectancy' of War) had a militaristic regime. Arguably, the same could be said of Russia, once she recovered her strength. In Germany the military class had never really been suppressed. Britain and France had not seriously disarmed, though, paradoxically, they were not properly equipped either to carry out their obligations under the League Covenant or the Locarno treaties. At the same time, pacifist sentiment was growing in all countries, and Germany's Weimar Republic seemed to be settling down peaceably under the leadership of Stresemann.

It could well be argued then that at the end of the 'twenties the prospects for peace were relatively good. Some historians have argued that what altered this was the great series of world events which began to take effect just at this time.

Exercise 4

What is this great series of world events?

Figure 11   New York city-scene during the depression, 1929 (United Press International (UK)).

Specimen Answers

The great world economic crisis, touched off by the Wall Street crash of 1929 and culminating in general European crisis in 1931.

We now turn finally in this unit to the question of economic conditions, and their relationship to the First World War, and, of course, to the preliminary causation of the Second World War. With the help of Unit 20, the questions you will have to try to sort out for yourselves are:

1   Would peace have been preserved without the great economic crisis, or was the legacy of the First World War such that 'international instability' was bound to bring further war sooner or later?

2   Or is this an unreal question in that the economic crisis itself was a direct result either of the war, or of the Versailles settlement, or both?

3   Even given the great economic crisis was it still possible for peace to be preserved in the 1930s?

19.3   POST-WAR DEPRESSION AND THE ANALOGUE OF WAR

Now read *Roberts*, Chapter XI, pages 343–67. The first question we have to address ourselves to concerns the causation of the widespread economic depression of the post-war years which culminated in the great crisis of 1929–31. Is the depression related to the war itself, or to the peace settlement or was it caused by altogether different factors? Using the materials supplied by Roberts, and applying my ideas of *destruction and disruption, test,* and *psychological effects* (see Unit 2, Section 2.2) I think one can establish a relationship between the war itself and the depression. An older school of critics of the Versailles settlement like to blame it, and in particular the Reparations clauses. Undoubtedly Reparations were a symptom of a wider policy of economic nationalism stirred up by the war, but, although they were important in continuing German bitterness, they were not in the end actually economically significant.

Exercise 1

As appropriate, note against each of the three tiers of the War and Social Change model mentioned above (*destruction, test, psychological*) points which Roberts uses to explain the economic depression.

Specimen Answers

Destruction and disruption

Fragmentation of the old economic system (p. 343). Damage done to the International Monetary System (p. 345). The elaborate but smooth channels of pre-war international payments disrupted and jammed (p. 345). The physical damage of war (p. 345). Exhaustion of London gold reserves (p. 348). Demographic losses (p. 352). Large-scale migrations (p. 352). Extra European markets had often been disrupted during the war (p. 361). Wartime disruption of normal trade (p. 364). Brutal readjustment to peace after wartime industrial expansion (p. 365).

Test

War exposed the contingent quality of economic thought and institutions of pre-war years (p. 344).

Psychological effects

Growth of economic nationalism leading to 'policies of withdrawal and insulation'. (p. 343)

Exercise 2

What points made by Roberts associate the depression with causes other than the war?

Specimen Answer

The main points are that decline of population growth had already set in before the war; that nineteenth-century economic expansion was already losing its impetus before the war; that new technological developments affected the prosperity of coal producing areas, etc.; above all the point that the pre-war system was 'contingent' suggests that it might well have been due for collapse anyway, even without the war.

We might then conclude that the war did have a considerable effect in bringing about the depression as an actual historical circumstance, but that other causes contributed to it as well.

Still on this point, take a look at the indices of industrial production quoted by Roberts in footnote 3 on page 349, and read them in conjunction with what he says in his last paragraph on that page.

Exercise 3

What conclusions might one draw from the table about the correlation between the war and industrial depression?

Specimen Answer

The least depressed country was Sweden, which was a neutral in the war. Next comes Britain, which, at least, did not suffer invasion. The worst-off country is Germany, which of course was defeated in the war. In other words this *might* suggest that the greater the direct impact of war, the more intense the effects of economic depression. (I italicize *might* because of course this is a too facile conclusion to draw from these few figures alone.)

Exercise 5

Did the new economic experiments of the war provide examples which could be used to rescue the various countries from the worst effects of economic depression? Answer this first of all on the basis of your reading in Roberts.

Figure 12   Unemployed in the Weimar Republic (Staatsbibliothek Berlin. Preussicher Kulturbesitz Bildarchiv. Photo: Herbert Hoffmann).

Specimen Answer

Very briefly at the foot of page 366 and the top of page 367 Roberts refers to growing government intervention in the economy, Keynesian thinking and so on, and remarks that 'the Great War heralded a much more profound change in thinking; its interferences with property went further than ever before and many of them were permanent.'

On the other hand, recalling from the table of indices of industrial production that Sweden suffered least and recovered most, one might argue that on the contrary it was the country without the experience of war which most quickly found the means to overcome economic depression.

Exercise 6

Now read, or re-read Leuchtenburg's article 'The New Deal and the Analogue of War' (Unit 16). Summarize in two or three sentences his argument about the effects of war in solving the economic depression.

Specimen Answers

Leuchtenburg shows how most of the ideas for combating the depression through the New Deal came from the example and experience of the war. But in the end, says Leuchtenburg, the New Deal would have been much more effective if its organizers had gone straight to the roots of the economic and social problems they were supposed to be dealing with, instead of seeking refuge in the analogue of war.

Leuchtenburg, of course, is concerned over the specially strong *laissez-faire* attitudes prevalent in the United States, and he is criticizing a situation in which reluctance to resort to national collectivist action could not be overcome without resorting to the phraseology of war.

None the less, recalling the Swedish situation which we highlighted above, one might argue that 'The Analogue of War' was misleading in the search for economic recovery in the inter-war years. You may possibly be aware that it is often argued that Sweden was most successful in solving the problems of inter-war capitalism in crisis. Perhaps this was because, not having participated in the previous war, Sweden was not misled by the analogue of war.

This, I would think, would be a very bold generalization to draw from very inadequate evidence. However, I present it to you here, partly as an antidote to my own theories, and more critically to stress once again the very complexity of historical processes. If you are baffled, think of it like this: when the great economic crisis (which may or may not have been caused by the war) came, politicians sought remedies in the economic experiments of the war ('the analogue of war'), but perhaps if they had ignored the war they would have come up with better remedies, as Sweden seems to have done (or perhaps, of course, they wouldn't have come up with any remedies at all!).

Now, if you still have time in hand, carry on with your reading of Taylor.

Note on Books

There are adequate bibliographies in Taylor (at the end) and in Roberts (at the beginning of Chapter X). To the books mentioned there add the ones by Hinsley, Medlicott, and Northedge referred to in the course of the unit (see page 19).

ACKNOWLEDGEMENTS

Grateful acknowledgement is made to the following for material used in this unit:

TEXT

Longman Group, Ltd. for J. M. Roberts, *Europe 1880–1945*; Penguin Books Ltd. for A. J. P. Taylor, *Origins of the Second World War*.

ILLUSTRATIONS

Associated Press; Mansell Collection; Philadelphia Museum of Art; Carl Zigrasser Collection; Staatsbibliothek Berlin, Preussischer Kulturbesitz Bildarchiv; United Press International (UK).

The map on page 15 is from *The Origins of the Second World War* by A. J. P. Taylor. Copyright © 1961 by A. J. P. Taylor. Reprinted by permission of Hamish Hamilton, London and Atheneum Publishers, New York, N.Y.

Unit 20

The Origins of World War II

Prepared for the Course Team by Anthony Adamthwaite,
Lecturer in History, School of European Studies,
University of Bradford

CONTENTS AND OBJECTIVES

Note on Reading

In addition to the correspondence material and the radio discussion you are asked to make a careful and critical reading of A. J. P. Taylor's *The Origins of the Second World War* (2nd edition, with the Foreword: 'Second Thoughts'). This is the edition cited in the unit and it forms the basis of the radio programme; it is essential that you use it.

As a general set textbook you are already familiar with J. M. Roberts, *Europe, 1880–1945*. Recommended as supplementary reading is *The Origins of the Second World War*, edited by Esmonde M. Robertson. This is an extremely useful collection of essays, reprinted from various journals. It contains a very important article by Dr Tim Mason of St Antony's College, Oxford, who is one of the participants in the radio programme. The article is entitled 'Some Origins of the Second World War' (pp. 105–35). Reprinted with it is a reply from A. J. P. Taylor: 'War Origins Again' (pp. 136–41).

You were introduced to Taylor's *Origins* last week, but it may be helpful here to say a further brief word about this book. A. J. P. Taylor, one of the most distinguished of contemporary British historians, is doubtless well known to you. Even if you have not read him, you have probably watched some of his television programmes and you will be listening to him in the radio programme. His *Origins*, first published in 1961, gave rise to some acrimonious polemics, and some of the articles reprinted in Esmonde Robertson's collection will give you a measure of the feelings aroused in some critics. The dust has now settled on these disputes and *Origins* stands as a brilliant and original contribution to the subject. In recent years there has been a steady flow of monographs and articles on the subject of war origins but no other historian has yet attempted to write a general interpretation of events on the scale of *Origins*. Nevertheless, Taylor's book must be read in the light of recent researches and one objective of this unit is to provide you with a framework of reference. To get the feel, so to speak, of Taylor I suggest that you read him through at one sitting, perhaps making the occasional note as you go along. Before starting the unit it might be worth while to refresh your memory of Professor Marwick's summary of the debate on the origins of World War II in Chapter 7 of *The Nature of History* (pp. 235–9).

20.1 THE IMPORTANCE OF THE SUBJECT

20.1.1 The Second World War needs no introduction. Both world wars have captured the popular imagination, though, as a student of the Second World War, perhaps I may be forgiven for arguing that the Second conflict exercises a greater fascination than the First. The survivors of the Somme are now in old age and memories of the trenches are fast fading into history. Not so experiences of the blitz, evacuation and rationing, which are shared by many. Indeed, if the popularity of the television series 'Dad's Army' is any guide, we are still fighting the war of 1939–45. Interest in the war is not peculiar to one generation; in fact, the family is at war.

None the less, a unit devoted to the origins of World War II may possibly occasion some surprise. To many, the origins of the war present no mystery. If historians were to hold a public opinion poll and ask who was responsible for the outbreak of the war, the overwhelming answer would probably be: Adolf Hitler. All that such a poll would reveal is the often considerable time-lag between popular opinion on a subject and specialist research. Today, historians would see the question of war origins in rather different terms, though fifteen or so years ago they would have said that only one cause really mattered—Hitler. When *Origins* first appeared in 1961, Taylor spoke of an 'almost universal agreement among historians' on the causes of the war. In an introduction to *Hitler's War Directives*, Professor H. R. Trevor-Roper wrote of the outbreak of the war: Hitler 'intended it, he prepared for it, he chose the moment for launching it' (p. xiii). In fact both historians and the general public were agreed in drawing a sharp contrast between the origins of the Second World War and those of the First. There was a general feeling that while in 1914 'the nations' in Lloyd George's phrase, 'slithered over the brink into the cauldron of war', in 1939, war was the deliberate design of one man, Hitler.

The view that Hitler and his immediate advisers planned and unleashed the war of 1939–45 was orthodox opinion in the late 1940s and 1950s. If the question of secondary responsibilities arose, then the Germans themselves were often branded as troublemakers. Of course, this was nothing new. In Unit 14 Professor Marwick pointed out that at the end of the First World War the victorious allies pinned blame for the war firmly and definitely on Germany. In 1945 belief in Hitler's personal responsibility for war was underpinned by some very crude stereotypes of German character and history. Maybe you have read *The Rise and Fall of the Third Reich* by the American historian, William L. Shirer, who worked as a journalist in Germany in the 1930s. The huge success of that book is partly to be explained by the fact that the author pandered to popular prejudice in presenting 'Nazism as a logical continuation of German history'. According to Shirer, Hitler may have started the war of 1939, but if he had not done so Germany would have gone to war sooner or later.

However, the consensus that the primary responsibility for the outbreak of war rested on Hitler and the Nazis did not stifle historical debate and research. On the contrary, there remained considerable scope for speculation as to the parts played by other powers in the coming of war. Great Britain and France were given bad marks for their policy of appeasement and for their failure to reach agreement with the Soviet Union in the summer of 1939. Winston Churchill and his followers who had criticized the policy of appeasement in 1938–9 claimed that the war was an unnecessary one. Hitler, it was argued, could have been stopped without war if the government of the day had displayed greater resolution and firmness. Churchill's outlook was reflected in his war memoirs, *The Second World War*. His thesis was also shared by a leading British historian, Sir Lewis Namier, who contributed three works to a study of the origins of the war: *Diplomatic Prelude* (1948); *Europe in Decay* (1950); *In the Nazi Era* (1952). In the discussion of war origins both the Poles and the Russians came in for their share of criticism: the Poles, for the illusion that they could somehow keep both the Soviet Union and Germany at a safe distance; the Russians, for the Nazi–Soviet Pact of 23 August 1939. Nor did the Italian dictator, Benito Mussolini, escape scot-free. It was suggested that if Italy had refused to conclude the Pact of Steel with Germany on 22 May 1939, then Hitler might have thought twice before attacking Poland in September.

One major feature of the conventional wisdom which prevailed in the matter of war origins was the belief that from the causes of the war of 1939–45 one could draw a valuable lesson about the origins of war in general. In the opinion of statesmen and public alike the moral to be drawn from the conflict was that appeasement ends in disaster. A leading exponent of this philosophy was Lord Avon who, as Sir Anthony Eden, served as Foreign Secretary first to Neville Chamberlain, until February 1938, and then to Churchill from 1942 to 1945 and again from 1951 to 1955. Lord Avon always maintained, and the titles of his three volumes of memoirs (*Full Circle*, *Facing the Dictators*, *The Reckoning*) pointed his view, that his actions and decisions in the late 1950s, particularly in the Suez crisis of 1956, were decisively shaped by his judgement of what ought to have been done in the 1930s. As Prime Minister in 1956, Lord Avon thought he saw in the régime of Colonel Nasser of Egypt a repetition of Hitler's Third Reich. Appeasement of the dictators in the 1930s had seemed to lead to war and disaster but Avon's determination not to repeat past mistakes produced another disaster, even if a relatively minor one, in the Suez intervention of October 1956. Similarly, in the early 1950s, the attitude of the American Secretary of State, John Foster Dulles, was strongly influenced by a determination not to 'appease' the Soviet Union. Here it must be stressed that the word appeasement was a perfectly respectable and honourable term in the diplomatic vocabulary of the 1930s, at least until the Munich crisis of September 1938. As originally employed by Neville Chamberlain and his colleagues the term denoted a diplomacy of conciliation and accommodation. By 1939–40, however, appeasement signified almost exclusively a policy of retreat, surrender and betrayal. Like the word 'Fascist', 'appeaser' became a convenient smear word in politics. Condemnation of appeasement in this pejorative sense was one of the shibboleths of post-1945 international politics. The climax of Chamberlain's diplomacy was marked by the Munich Agreement of 30 September 1938 by which the four European powers, Great Britain, France, Germany and Italy, settled the problem of Czechoslovakia. After the Cuban missile crisis of October 1962 the then Prime Minister, Mr Harold Macmillan, praised President Kennedy of the United States for having avoided a 'super-Munich'. Thus Munich and appeasement in the nasty sense had become virtually synonymous. Fortunately, historians, unlike statesmen, have generally resisted the temptation to draw far-reaching conclusions from particular events or situations.

It is tempting to link together the two world wars and see them as part of one vast European civil war which raged from 1905 to 1945. In Unit 14 Professor Marwick drew your attention to Taylor's stress in *Origins* on the continuity of German history; both wars, according to Taylor, were the product of Germany's drive for domination. Taylor argues that the Second World War grew out of the First. The peace settlement which followed the war of 1914–18 left German unity intact and thereby sowed the seeds of future conflict. But the novelty of *Origins* did not lie in the firm statement of the continuity of recent Germany history but in the interpretation of Hitler's personality and policy. Hitler, it is suggested, was a supreme opportunist who had few, if any, long-term objectives. As Taylor says in the radio discussion which accompanies this unit: Hitler's 'goal . . . the only goal' was

34

'success'. Again, to quote *Origins*, Hitler 'did not so much aim at war as expect it to happen' (p. 12). If this thesis about Hitler is accepted, then the war had really 'little to do with Hitler' and the 'vital question' is why Great Britain and France failed to resist Germany before 1939.

Taylor's questioning of established thinking was not entirely new; for some time scholars had been scrutinizing some of the wider issues which shaped international affairs between the two world wars; the disagreements which troubed Anglo-French relations, the retreat of the United States into isolation, the exclusion of the Soviet Union, the social consequences of the Great Depression. Nevertheless, the impact of *Origins* owed much to the fact that for the first time the different strands of scholarship were drawn together into a sustained piece of writing.

Taylor's thesis struck at the heart of the accepted version of events. The centrepiece of the accepted version was a view of Hitler as a megalomaniac, who with unwavering villainy, initiated and pursued a programme of world conquest, first propounded in *Mein Kampf* in 1924, and confirmed upon his advent to power in 1933. Given this picture of Hitler as a fanatic intent on war, the allocation of responsibility for the outbreak of the war was an easy task, and in comparison to the role of Hitler, the contribution of other statesmen and issues was entirely secondary. Taylor, in stressing the German leader's opportunism and in suggesting that in international affairs there was little to choose between him and other statesmen, shifted the focus of interest and enquiry to the other powers.

To sum up: it is evident that the view of the origins of the Second World War which prevailed some fifteen to twenty years ago can no longer be maintained intact. The operative word is 'intact'. Historians have not radically altered their way of looking at the origins of the war. Hitler's evil genius has not been conjured away. His role as chief villain is not in dispute. The generality of opinion would not accept the thesis of *Origins* that the war of 1939 was the result of blunder and miscalculation. However, it is accepted that Hitler did not want a European war in 1939, let alone a world war. In short, Hitler wanted a war with Poland but not a war with the Western powers. If the general picture is relatively clear, though blurred at the edges, there is a mass of detail to fill in. The British and French governments have replaced the traditional fifty-year rules of access to official papers by a thirty-year rule. A great quantity of material for the 1930s and the Second World War is now open to inspection. This is in addition to the hundreds of tons of German documents of the Third Reich which the allies captured in 1945. The sifting of the recently-released British and French papers will occupy historians for a long time. Questions such as Germany's economic situation in the 1930s, the state of German armaments under Hitler, the institutional structure of the Third Reich, the interplay of foreign and domestic policies in Britain and France, have been comparatively neglected and this whole subject of war origins, as you will see from a glance at Esmonde Robertson's collection of articles, is very much a matter of continuing research and enquiry.

Exercise 1

In the light of the foregoing, say what sort of views about the Second World War and its origins underlie the following passages.

A   The end came with grave serenity this afternoon. Within a brief hour the International Military Tribunal, speaking in the name of the civilised world, has passed sentence on the convicted leaders of Nazi Germany and, its findings implemented by the austere authority of the law, Nuremberg passed into history.

Eleven of the 21 prisoners, including Hermann Goering, and the soldiers Keitel and Jodl, were sentenced to death by hanging, with a twelfth death sentence recorded in the case of the absent Martin Bormann. Raeder, the Grand Admiral, Rudolf Hess, and Funk . . . were sent to prison for life, and four more received such sentences of from 10 to 20 years' imprisonment. Such are the dire penalties exacted from chiefs of state and military leaders for all the blood and all the unholiness in which they engulfed their generation by the crime of aggressive war.

B   Never had an aggressor made his ambitions known more plainly beforehand, never had a party more repeatedly and consistently given warning of what it proposed to attempt. It was all set out in *Mein Kampf* in 1924, in the party programme, in the speeches and writing of the leaders and above all of Hitler himself. . . . Just as the Nazis grew in strength and captured power in Germany because few took them seriously and some hoped to outwit them, so Nazi Germany came to dominate Europe because civilised men could not believe that so monstrous a regime could exist or succeed. It was overlooked that the resources of power at the disposal of any government of a great modern industrial state are imponderable, and that power, made almost absolute, becomes absolutely corrupting. The Second World War began as the first brave concerted effort of Europe's two oldest nations to defy and destroy this power.

C   In the Europe of the 1930s there were several leaders—Mussolini, for example—who would have liked to follow such a policy, but lacked the toughness of will and the means to carry it through. Hitler alone possessed the will and had provided himself with the means. Not only did he create the threat of war and exploit it, but when it came to the point he was prepared to take the risk and go to war and, then when he had won the Polish campaign, to redouble the stakes and attack again, first in the West, then in the East. For this reason, despite all that we have learned since of the irresolution, shabbiness, and chicanery of other governments' policies, Hitler and the nation which followed him still bear, not the sole, but the primary responsibility for the war which began in 1939 and which, before Hitler was prepared to admit defeat, cost the lives of more than 25 million human beings in Europe alone.

D   One day President Roosevelt told me that he was asking publicly for suggestions about what the war should be called. I said at once 'the Unnecessary War'. There never was a war more easy to stop than that which has just wrecked what was left of the world from the previous struggle.

E   The issue of a crisis depends not so much on its magnitude as on the courage and resolution with which it is met. The second German bid for world domination found Europe weak and divided. At several junctures it could have been stopped without excessive effort or sacrifice, but was not: a failure of European statesmanship. Behind the German drive were passionate forces, sustained by obsessionist, sadistic hatreds and by a crude ideology; to these the Germans, whom defeat had deprived of their routine of life, showed even more than their normal receptivity, while the rest of Europe had neither the faith, nor the will, nor even sufficient repugnance, to offer timely, effective resistance. Some imitated Hitler and hyena-like followed in his track; some tolerated him hoping that his advance would reach its term—by saturation, exhaustion, the resistance of others, or the mere chapter of accidents—before it attained them; and some, while beholding his handiwork, would praise him for having 'restored the self-respect of the Germans'. Janissaries and appeasers aided Hitler's work: a failure of European morality.

F   Another factor of decisive importance which helped to unleash Hitler's aggression was the policy of the ruling circles of England and France which is known as the policy of 'appeasing' Hitler Germany, a policy of renouncing collective security . . . it should be clear to everyone that this policy of British and French ruling circles . . . led to the Second World War. . . . As far back as 1937 it became perfectly clear that a great war was being hatched by Hitler with the direct connivance of Great Britain and France.

G   German thought and German practice have for the last century and a half been undermining the civilisation of the west; they are hostile to that civilisation and eager to bring about its ruin; they wish its ruin because it is built upon the mean of reason, the christian ethic, the scientific spirit, and human worth—all alien to the German outlook, which casts back to barbarism. . . . German thought has come to deny the very value of human life within the concord of oecumenical society, holding that right order is only to be achieved by cultivation of the brutishness of tribal man and his worship of the tribal totem. Here civilisation is confronted face to face with barbarism. Now it is one against the other, and the fight is to the death.

H   My book has really little to do with Hitler. The vital question, it seems to me, concerns Great Britain and France. They were the victors of the First World War. They had the decision in their hands. It was perfectly obvious that Germany would seek to become a Great Power again; obvious after 1933 that her domination would be of a peculiarly barbaric sort. Why did the victors not resist her?...

Discussion

A   This passage, describing the verdict of the International Military Tribunal at Nuremberg in 1946, vividly conveys the sense of moral outrage which governed attitudes towards Germany in the immediate aftermath of war. Of course, many Germans no doubt drew their own conclusions from the bombing of Dresden and Hiroshima. It comes from *The Times* of 2 October 1946.

B   This passage, concerned with the origins of the war, takes a broad look at the subject. While the primary responsibility is assigned to Hitler and Nazism, other more impersonal forces are hinted at in the reference to the power of the modern industrial State. The author of the passage makes it clear that in his view German aggression was premeditated. The moral tone, so evident in the first passage, is still strong. Britain and France were the brave nations who defied Germany. The extract comes from a standard textbook of nineteenth- and twentieth-century European history, *Europe since Napoleon*, by David Thomson (Penguin Books, 1966, pp. 758–9). It sums up quite neatly the prevailing outlook among historians in the 1940s and 1950s.

C   This third passage, also concerned with the origins of the war, is noteworthy as a recent restatement of the orthodox version of events. It comes from the pen of Alan Bullock, author of the standard English biography of Hitler.[1] The Raleigh Lecture of 1967, from which this extract is taken, is reprinted in Esmonde M. Robertson, *The Origins of the Second World War* (pp. 189–221).

D   Here is a succinct statement of Winston Churchill's conviction that the war could have been prevented. It comes from the preface to volume I of his war memoirs, *The Gathering Storm* (Cassell, 1948).

E   This extract provides a neat summary of the opinions of an eminent British historian who held similar views to those of Churchill. The passage is significant because although written in the wake of war it yet offers a sophisticated statement of the origins of the conflict. It comes from Sir Lewis Namier's *Diplomatic Prelude, 1938–1939* (Macmillan, 1948), page ix. Namier's approach has rather fallen out of favour but his argument in this passage merits close reading. Namier, it seems to me, is saying in 1948 very much what Taylor said in *Origins* thirteen years later. Namier is not content with the simple explanation that Hitler's will alone caused the war, though he clearly believes that Hitler's was the primary impulse to war. He suggests in fact that a large share of responsibility rests with Germany's opponents.

F   This is a crude statement of the Stalinist version of the outbreak of war. The whole burden of guilt is thrust firmly on Germany and the Western powers. It is argued that the war of 1939 was a capitalist plot aimed at directing Hitler against the Soviet Union. But this extract was also the product of another conflict, the propaganda campaign of the Cold War between the Soviet Union and the West which set in quickly after 1945. The half-truths which underlie this document of the

[1] *Hitler: A Study in Tyranny*, Penguin Books, 1969.

Cold War require careful handling. It comes from an official Soviet publication, *Falsificators of History* (An Historical Note), Moscow, 1948, reprinted in *The Outbreak of the Second World War: Design or Blunder*, edited by John L. Snell (D. C. Heath, 1962), page 29.

G   This is a strongly anti-German view of the origins of the war. The previous extracts have roundly condemned Hitler and his advisers but not the German people and their history. It is a remarkable outburst of anti-Germanism, all the more remarkable because it was written by an academic historian, who later helped to edit the major official collection of foreign office papers *Documents on British Foreign Policy, 1919–1939* (London, H.M.S.O., 1949–). The author is Rohan D'Olier Butler and the extract is from his book *The Roots of National Socialism, 1783–1933* (Faber, 1941) page 297. Although published in wartime, the book was in fact planned before the outbreak of war.

H   This final passage marks a refreshing break from the moral judgements and preoccupation with Germany registered in the previous extracts. In assessing responsibility for the outbreak of war the emphasis has clearly shifted from Hitler to the other powers, principally Britain and France. It comes, as you should have realized, from Taylor's *Origins* (p. 9).

Exercise 2

There is no point in studying the origins of a war unless one has some understanding of its nature and results. No one would deny the importance of the Second World War but historians would differ in their estimates of its significance. Before embarking on an examination of the causes of the war, it might be a good idea to try to form some appreciation of the importance of the conflict. First read carefully what Roberts has to say in Chapter XVI, pp. 525–52. Read the chapter with two questions in mind: (1) what was the nature of the contest and how did it differ from the previous struggle? (2) what were the main results of the war? Make a note of the points which seem relevant to you. Then, after answering questions (1) and (2) read the two passages given below and say what you think of them in the light of your reading of Roberts (a brief paragraph on each passage should suffice).

A   The Second World War was, in large part, a repeat performance of the first. There were obvious differences. Italy fought on the opposite side, though she changed back again before the end. The war which began in September 1939, was fought in Europe and North Africa; it overlapped in time, though not in space, with the Far Eastern War, which began in December 1941. The two wars remained distinct, though the Far Eastern War created great embarrassments for Great Britain and the United States. Germany and Japan never joined forces; the only real overlap was when the Japanese attack on Pearl Harbour provoked Hitler, very mistakenly, to declare war on the United States. Otherwise the European war and its origin can be treated as a story in itself, the Far East providing occasional distractions off-stage. In the Second World War approximately the same European allies fought approximately the same adversaries as in the first. Though the tide of battle swung more violently to and fro, the war ended in much the same way—with the defeat of Germany. The link between the two wars went deeper. Germany fought specifically in the second World War to reverse the verdict of the first and to destroy the settlement which followed it. Her opponents fought, though less consciously, to defend that settlement; and this they achieved—to their own surprise. There was much Utopian projecting while the war was on; but at the end virtually every frontier in Europe and the Near East was restored unchanged, with the exception—admittedly a large exception—of Poland and the Baltic. Leaving out this area of north-eastern Europe, the only serious change on the map between the English Channel and the Indian Ocean was the transference of Istria from Italy to Yugoslavia. The first war destroyed old empires and brought new states into existence. The second war created no new states and destroyed only Estonia, Latvia and Lithuania. If one asks the rather crude question, 'what was the war about?', the answer for the first is: 'to decide how Europe should be remade', but for the second merely: 'To decide whether this remade Europe should continue'. . . .

B   Yet the obvious similarities should not obscure the equally significant differences. The second was much more truly than the first a world war, for it saw prolonged fighting in the Pacific as well as in the Atlantic, in Asia and Africa as well as in Europe, the defeat of Japan as well as of Germany and Italy. It brought the collapse not of Russia but of France, revolution not in Russia but in China, the partition not of Turkey and Austria-Hungary but of Germany itself. The greatest similarity between the two wars was that the eventual outcome of each was quite unforeseen and largely unintended when it began : their main historical significance lies in what the course of events itself led to, rather than the planned objectives of any belligerent.

Again it is especially important for the aftermath of the war to be considered in the closest possible relation to the course of the war itself. If the period of settlement after 1918 must properly be regarded as lasting at least five years after the end of hostilities, the period of settlement after 1945—as befits the aftermath of a war which lasted half as long again and extended over a much larger area of the world—must be regarded as lasting for at least a decade after the end of hostilities. The aftermath included a sequence of secondary wars—wars in Palestine, in Indo-China, in Korea, in Algeria—all of which were part of the same great story. It included, too, a series of revolutions, in the internal structure of western European states, in the connexions between these states and their colonial territories, and in the whole fabric of international relations and organisations. These revolutions had taken clearer if not final shape by 1960. For all these reasons the second great era of 'War and Peace' in twentieth-century Europe must be regarded as extending from 1939 to 1960.

Specimen Answer

List of points from Roberts

(1)   What was the nature of the war and how did it differ from the previous conflict?

(i)   Basically the same struggle as that of 1914–18, the overcoming of Germany (p. 525).

(ii)   Reassertion of offensive power over defensive strength (p. 526).

(iii)   Major technical innovations: radar, pilotless and rocket missiles and jet-propelled aircraft (p. 526).

(iv)   Total subordination of economy and society to war effort in Great Britain and Soviet Union, Germany much slower to organize a full war economy. These developments foreshadowed by experiences of 1914–18.

(v)   Ideological nature of contest—'Nazism was the worst challenge ever presented to liberal civilisation' (p. 540). This feature was not present in 1914–18.

(vi)   Resistance movements in Hitler's Europe, requiring deployment of large numbers of German forces, especially in France and Yugoslavia. Again this is a feature peculiar to 1939–45 war (p. 539).

(2)   What were the main results of the war?

(i)   Complete destruction of Germany as a great Power. Defeat of 1945 much more thorough than that of 1918 (pp. 540, 548).

(ii)   Eclipse of economic, political and military power of European states: dominance in Europe of two non-European military powers, United States and Soviet Union (pp. 548–9).

(iii)   Complete restoration of Russia as a leading great power, her influence in 1945 much greater than in 1914 or 1939 (p. 548).

(iv)   Re-establishment of France (p. 547).

(v)   Restoration of European colonial empires in Asia and Far East but, in contrast to 1918, there was no extension of colonial territories. Moreover, European restoration in Asia was extremely precarious as a result of Japanese conquests (p. 549).

(vi) Demographic losses (p. 538).

Some of the points which I have listed you may not have thought important, though on the whole we should both have covered similar ground. For example, you may not have thought (1) (vi) worth noting. However, if you missed (1) (i), (ii), (iv), then perhaps you should re-read the chapter. Naturally, the lists are not exhaustive. I have confined myself to Roberts, though certainly under (2) one ought to add as a separate point the defeat of Japan and her loss of empire.

Discussion

The first passage comes, as you probably realized, from Taylor's *Origins* (p. 41) and the second from David Thomson's *Europe since Napoleon* (pp. 763–4). The viewpoint of A is plainly stated in the opening sentence and what follows is an attempt to sustain the argument that the Second World War was a 'repeat perform-ance' of the First. My comment is that the author is really stretching the argument further than the evidence would warrant. His stance is too narrowly European. Consequently, the extra-European or world-wide nature of the conflict is unduly minimized. This distortion is shown in the passing references to the Far East. Actually, the role of Japan rather weakens the author's thesis since Japan fought against Germany in 1914–18. While it is true that the United States and Great Britain gave priority to the war in Europe, Japanese conquests in the Far East irreparably damaged European prestige. The fall of Singapore in February 1942 was the greatest capitulation in British military history. Again, the sins of omission are numerous; for instance, nothing is said of the role of resistance movements in occupied Europe and of their significance for post-war politics, nor of the ideological threat of Nazism, nor of the demographic losses sustained. While there are no generally accepted casualty figures for either of the world wars, Gordon Wright, in his book *The Ordeal of Total War, 1939–1945* (another set book for this course, which you will be reading in conjunction with the next block of units) estimates that 'the dead in Europe approximated 30 millions—a half again as great as that of the First World War' (p. 263). As for the political results of the war, Taylor paints a rather misleading picture. He writes 'at the end virtually every frontier in Europe and the Near East was restored unchanged, with the exception—admit-tedly a large exception—of Poland and the Baltic.' It might be said that the exception is so large as to invalidate the generalization. Here, in my opinion, Roberts is a surer guide. Granted that the war created no new States, it did destroy Japan as a military power. Italy, too, lost both monarchy and empire. Perhaps enough has been said to show that passage A is open to serious criticism.

Passage B is much more concerned to bring out the differences between the two wars. On the whole, I would agree with Thomson's verdict that the 'second was much more truly than the first a world war.' But you may have noticed that the second half of the passage does not hang together particularly well. It is not made clear how the war influenced developments up to 1955 or 1960. If Taylor looks at the war of 1939–45 too much from the vantage point of the previous struggle, Thomson looks too far ahead and loses a certain amount of historical perspective.

Last Comment

Roberts, in his discussion of the military characteristics of the Second World War, does not mention the development and harnessing for military purposes of atomic energy, perhaps because it did not affect the war in Europe. Nevertheless, the breakthrough in the development of atomic energy constituted a major qualitative difference, dividing the war of 1939–45 not only from the Great War but from all previous conflicts. In the words of Gordon Wright, the military use of atomic energy was the Second World War's 'principal contribution to the future, ensuring that there would never be another conflict on the lines of 1939–1945' (*The Ordeal of Total War*, p. 106). The dropping of the atomic bomb on the city of Hiroshima on 6 August 1945 marked the start of a new age in international relations, still recognizably our own, in which the existence of a relatively stable 'balance of terror' has prevented the outbreak of a third world war. The novelist Arthur Koestler sums up forcefully the reality which is too much for most of us to bear:

All comparisons with past epochs break down before the fact that our species has acquired the means to annihilate itself, and make the earth uninhabitable; and that in the foreseeable future, it will be within its power to turn the planet into a nova, a rival sun in the solar system.

(*The Sleepwalkers: A History of Man's Changing Vision of The Universe*, Penguin Books, 1964, p. 551.)

In 'Dirge for the New Sunrise' (1945) Edith Sitwell supplied a poetic statement of this nightmarish situation:

> . . . But I saw the little Ant-men as they ran
> Carrying the world's weight of the world's filth
> And the filth in the heart of Man—
> Compressed till those lusts and greeds had a greater heat
>   than that of the Sun.
> And the ray from that heat came soundless, shook the sky
> As if in search of food, and squeezed the stems
> Of all that grows on the earth till they were dry
> —And drank the marrow of the bone:
> The eyes that saw, the lips that kissed, are gone
> Or black as thunder lie and grin at the murdered Sun . . .

('Three Poems of the Atomic Age' in *Collected Poems*, Macmillan, 1965, p. 369.)

20.2 THE CAUSES OF THE SECOND WORLD WAR

20.2.1   In analysing the origins of the war one can draw an obvious distinction between the immediate and the deeper causes of the conflict. The immediate causes are not in dispute. The German invasion of Poland on 1 September 1939 activated the British and French alliances with Poland and both powers declared war on Germany on 3 September. Thus the Second World War began as a European war between Great Britain, France and Poland on the one side, and Germany on the other. Italy did not enter the conflict until the following year. However, the immediate cause of a conflict tells little about its origins. Behind the German–Polish quarrel over Danzig and the Polish Corridor lay deeper causes about which historians differ. It would be quite misleading of me to present you with a neat package of causes. Instead, I have mapped out area by area the ground over which any discussion must range. I have listed, as a basis for discussion, eight topics.

1   'International instability'

The 'international instability' of the period after 1918 has been seen as one of the determining causes of the Second World War. In Unit 19 Professor Marwick told you that the Cambridge historian, Professor F. H. Hinsley, lays special emphasis on this feature of post-Versailles Europe. To exemplify this instability historians point to the shortcomings of the peace settlement and to the survival of the 'German problem'. Some historians, especially Taylor in *Origins*, would, as you saw in Unit 19, talk of a complete disruption of the balance of power. The United States and Russia had withdrawn from Europe, France was much weakened by the war of 1914–18.

2 Anglo-French policy

The policies pursued by Great Britain and France were clearly of profound importance. You will have noted that Taylor says that the origins have really little to do with Hitler and the 'vital question' was why Great Britain and France failed to resist Germany. There is much to be said for the view that if Britain and France, the principal victors of 1918, had agreed on a common policy towards Germany, the so-called 'German problem' might have been controlled and a second European

Figure 1 'Our last hope—Hitler', *National Socialist poster (Imperial War Museum)*.

conflict averted. As events turned out, the peace settlement was wrecked on the rock of Anglo-French disunity. In the immediate post-war period France wanted to enforce the peace treaties, lock, stock and barrel, while Britain sought to exercise a moderating influence, aimed at restoring Germany to the concert of European powers. After 1931, both countries increasingly sought to conciliate Germany and some historians would argue that this policy of appeasement only served to encourage German ambitions and brought into the open the latent instability of the international system.

3   Effects of the Great Depression

The social and economic effects of the Great Depression which engulfed Europe after 1929 had, it is suggested, a far-reaching influence on events. In Germany, thanks to unemployment, the National Socialists became a major political force, and some would argue that but for the Depression Hitler would never have achieved power. In Britain and France the effects of the Depression conditioned the formulation of foreign policy. The interaction between domestic and foreign problems determined reactions to Hitler's expansionist ambitions.

4   Hitler and National Socialism

Hitler and his ideology of National Socialism obviously played some part in the causation of war, but historians differ in their interpretation of Hitler's aims and ideas. However, most historians today would agree that while Hitler did not want a European war in 1939, none the less his aims and methods were warlike and a collision between Germany and other powers was only a matter of time. Most historians, too, would wish to stress the driving force of Nazi ideology, viz., the basic ideas of *Lebensraum*—the drive for living-space in the east, racialism, especially its anti-semitic aspects, anti-Bolshevism, the destruction of the Versailles peace settlement. Some writers, notably Dr Tim Mason, would go further in emphasizing the ideological framework of German policy. In particular, Dr Mason, as the radio programme indicates, argues that by 1939 the economic, political and social tensions in Hitler's Reich had grown to such a point that war seemed the only remedy. By contrast, Taylor contends that Hitler was little motivated by ideological considerations. Hitler, he argues, did not want war in 1939 and the outbreak of war was the result of misunderstandings and miscalculations.

5   Ideological divisions

The deeply-felt ideological disagreements which characterized the inter-war years were significant in two ways. In the first place the clash of ideologies—Left versus Right, Liberals versus Totalitarians—poisoned the climate of international relations and reduced the prospects of international understanding; in the second, while the ideologies of Marxist–Leninism and Fascism had a cohesive effect in their countries of origin, they were a divisive force in the world at large, fomenting internal conflict and inhibiting a firm response to international perils.

6   Sociological factors

Here I would like to borrow a term used by Professor Marwick in Unit 14, *The Origins of the First World War*, namely the cluster of 'sociological factors', though as employed in this unit the label describes a different set of circumstances to those prevailing in the pre-1914 period. What I have in mind are the psychological effects of the First World War, firstly the universal detestation and horror of war, secondly the breakdown of accepted liberal values—a process which Roberts calls 'the shaking of liberal society'. In Unit 14 you saw how in the approach to 1914 'the will to war', so well exemplified in the literature of the time, helped to mould a climate of opinion which expected war and to some extent wanted it. By contrast in the 1920s and 1930s one can talk of a 'will to peace' and it is arguable that the profound pacifism which marked opinion in Britain, France and the United States prevented an effective response to the threats posed by Italy, Germany and Japan, thereby contributing to the growth of a warlike situation. The breakdown of accepted liberal values, as well as being a factor in the rise of the German and Italian dictatorships, left the two Western democracies, Britain and France, in a defensive, introspective state, ill-equipped to respond to the challenge of Fascism.

Hitler's Germany and Mussolini's Italy are an exception to this general 'will to peace', and extremely relevant here are some of the theories of the causes of war, examined in Unit 2, *Historical and Social Science Approaches*. Two papers in particular in the Bramson and Goethals collection, *War: Studies from Psychology, Sociology, Anthropology*, are particularly relevant: Gordon W. Allport's 'Role of Expectancy' and Durbin and Bowlby's 'Personal Aggressiveness and War'. It is worth while refreshing your memory of these ideas by re-reading pages 71–80 of Unit 2.

7   Economic causes

Economic causes, it is claimed, help to explain the outbreak of war in 1939. Firstly there are the arguments which were in vogue in the late 1930s, for example, the Marxist–Leninist thesis that capitalism inevitably leads to war. A more sophisticated version of this argument suggested that Nazism and Fascism represented the final aggressive stage of capitalism in decline and could only survive by war.

Another explanation which was popular on the eve of the war was the theory that Germany in 1939 was faced with a crisis of over-production—she had to win new markets or go to war. Secondly, there is the relatively recent school of thought, of which Dr Mason is a representative, which considers that economic considerations, along with other forces, contributed to the creation of a powerful drive to war in Germany in 1938–9.

8   Extra-European factors

Extra-European factors must be taken into account. The interaction between the problems of Europe and the rest of the world helped to build up international tensions and uncertainties. The First World War led to a diminution of the economic and political primacy of Europe. This erosion of European dominance made the two Western powers, Britain and France, extremely sensitive to extra-European considerations. In particular it created special problems for Great Britain since she tried to be both a European and a world power, an effort which was too much for her resources. The result of Japanese expansion in the 1930s was to induce in Britain and France a much greater readiness to compromise in Europe than would otherwise have been the case.

Exercise

Before discussing my eight topics in detail I would like you to read carefully and then comment on the following passages:

A   Wars are much like road accidents. They have a general cause and particular causes at the same time. Every road accident is caused in the last resort, by the invention of the internal combustion engine and by men's desire to get from one place to another. In this sense, the 'cure' for road accidents is to forbid motor-cars. But a motorist, charged with dangerous driving, would be ill-advised if he pleaded the existence of motor-cars as his sole defence. The police and the courts do not weigh profound causes. They seek a specific cause for each accident—error on the part of the driver; excessive speed; drunkenness; faulty brakes; bad road surface. So it is with wars.

'International anarchy' makes war possible; it does not make war certain. After 1918 more than one writer made his name by demonstrating the profound causes of the First World War; and, though the demonstrations were often correct, they thus diverted attention from the question why that particular war happened at that particular time. Both enquiries make sense on different levels. They are complementary, they do not exclude each other. The Second World War, too, had profound causes; but it also grew out of specific events, and these events are worth detailed examination.

(*Origins*, pp. 135–6.)

B   As the above quotation suggests, he is more interested, personally, in the specific events that led to the Second World War than in whatever may have been its profound causes. We cannot object on this score: 'both enquiries make sense on different levels.' But nobody, and least of all a man who recognises that both levels exist, can write a book on the origins of the Second World War without giving some attention to the profound causes. Mr Taylor duly, though somewhat perfunctorily, deals with them—or, rather, he deals with those 'profound causes' of the war that occupied the attention of the public at the time, and he discusses them only to dismiss them—quite rightly— as rubbish . . . however, Mr Taylor . . . takes up the position that, since these so-called 'profound causes' of the war are so much rubbish, the war had no profound causes at all. The remaining two thirds of his book are occupied with the details of the international crisis that took place between 1936 and 1939. There is hardly another word about anything except the specific incidents that led to the war. If the war had profound causes, as he has told us it did, we never learn what they were.

(F. H. Hinsley, *Power and the Pursuit of Peace*, Cambridge University Press, 1963, pp. 324–5.)

C   'The Second World War, too, had profound causes; but it also grew out of specific events, and these events are worth detailed examination.' Yet Mr Taylor's formula largely excludes the profound causes from consideration; it seems unable to accommodate political movements and ideologies. National Socialism was perhaps the profoundest cause of the Second World War, but Mr Taylor's book is not informed by any conception of the distinctive character and role of National Socialism in the history of twentieth century Europe.

(T. W. Mason, '*Some Origins of the Second World War*', in E. M. Robertson (ed.) *The Origins of the Second World War*, p. 106.)

Discussion

Passage A raises two issues: one, the usefulness of the road accident analogy in understanding the causes of war in general, the other the application of this insight to the causes of the Second World War. My own feeling is that the analogy hinders more than it helps. The general distinction between profound and particular causes is not particularly helpful in the sense in which they are used. It is partly a matter of definition. If by profound or general causes one understands the fundamental nature of man or the existence of sovereign national states then such categories are of little value in explaining the outbreak of a particular war since they explain everything and nothing. And Taylor does seem to understand profound causes in this sense. The analogy is both too simple and too mechanistic to serve as a model for such a complex phenomenon as war. Moreover, the rigid and narrow categorization of causes is a serious shortcoming. In Unit 2 Kenneth Thompson stressed that any adequate theory of the causes of war must be a 'multiple factor theory'. It follows that a model or illustration of the causes of war must be more complex and sophisticated than the one presented here.

Passages B and C both criticize Taylor's application of his formula of 'profound causes' to the origins of the Second World War, and I think the strictures are well-founded, though I would not accept entirely the observations in B. One obvious point which you will have noticed is how little space Taylor gives to an analysis of the 'profound causes'—a mere seven pages out of 336 pages of text (pp. 137–41). However, it is clear from Chapter 2 of *Origins* that Taylor believes there were some profound causes which did matter—the 'German problem' and the defects of the peace settlement. The trouble lies with Taylor's terminology which is too constricting and produces confusion. As Dr Tim Mason puts it: Taylor's own formula of 'profound causes' excludes the really profound causes from considera-tion. He then gives a specific example of a major force which Taylor neglects in his discussion (pp. 135–41) and says little of elsewhere in *Origins*. The statements that National Socialism was the 'profoundest cause' of the war would not command general assent, though many historians would accept that National Socialism was one of the profound or deeper causes. Dr Tim Mason's argument must not be confused with the general assertion that Fascism 'inevitably' produced war. Dr Mason suggests that National Socialism in combination with other factors produced a powerful expansionist dynamic in Hitler's Germany. The radio programme will have given you some idea of the difference in approach between the two historians.

20.2.2 What I propose to do next is to discuss in some detail my eight topics and to help you to form your own assessment of the arguments involved.

1   'International instability'

I have used the term 'international instability' to describe three related themes:

(i)   the disruption of the balance of power after 1918;
(ii)   the specific problems created by the post-World War I peace settlement;
(iii)   the survival of the 'German problem'.

Obviously the political reconstruction of Europe which took place from 1919 to 1923 contained elements of weakness but, in defence of the peacemakers, it might be said that it was no longer possible to create a self-contained European system, similar to that created by the Congress of Vienna in 1815. Possibly the dismember-ment of Germany which many Frenchmen wanted in 1919 might have led to a real balance of power but such a dismemberment was never practical politics in the circumstances of 1918–19.

Exercise 1a

According to *Origins*, the survival of the 'German problem' in a more acute form than before 1914 and the imposition on Germany of a peace treaty which many Germans and non-Germans regarded as unduly harsh made a second European conflict inevitable. What comments might be made on Taylor's weighting of these points?

Exercise 1b

What factors other than the peace settlement and the German problem contributed to the instability of post-1918 Europe?

Read *Taylor*, Chapter 2, and Chapter 10, pp. 267–9; also *Roberts*, pp. 368–75 and 322–4.

Specimen Answers

Exercise 1a

The argument of *Origins* is crystal-clear on this point. The Second World War 'had been implicit since the moment when the first war ended' (p. 336) and 'Germany fought specifically in the second World War to reverse the verdict of the first and to destroy the peace settlement which followed it' (p. 41).

The survival of Germany as a great power clearly represented a potential threat to international stability but I do not think it follows that a second European conflict was inevitable. It is well to recall some wise words of Roberts about the First World War: 'there was nothing unavoidable about the war until a comparatively late hour; accidents might have averted disaster at several "turning points" or crucial moments' (p. 239). What is worth emphasis is that by 1938 the Treaty of Versailles had been almost completely dismantled without war. The revision of the peace treaties had begun in the mid-1920s. From 1925 to 1932 France, spurred on by Britain, made a number of concessions, notably in reparations and in agreeing to withdraw her troops from the Rhineland five years before the expiry of the occupation. In other words, until Hitler's advent, it seemed possible that through patient, peaceful diplomacy, Germany would achieve her revisionist aims. It is worth bearing in mind that despite the serious unbalance there were a number of options available, and until 1936, or even 1938, the situation was still open-ended. Taylor's thesis leaves little scope for Hitler's contribution to events and one question which you must consider is whether the Second World War was caused not by the post-1918 unbalance but by Hitler's warlike ambitions which deliberately stretched the international system to breaking-point.

Exercise 1b

Taylor makes the following points:

the withdrawal of the United States and Russia from Europe;
the destruction of Austria-Hungary;
the exhaustion of France;
the economic growth in the 1920s and 1930s of the future super powers—the United States and the Soviet Union (p. 268);
Japan's dominance in the Far East (pp. 67–8).

Roberts covers the same ground but is much more explicit about the changed and changing position of Europe in the world. My comment is that Taylor's interpretation of the post-1918 international situation is much too Eurocentric. 'The history of Europe', he writes, 'revolved round "the German problem" ' (p. 66). This is true, yet the German problem would not have been so threatening but for the change in Europe's relationship with the world and the existence of sources of instability outside Europe. Taylor goes on to say that 'there was a second difference of great significance' between the Europe of 1914 and that of the inter-war years: 'Before 1914 the relations of the Great European Powers had often been shaped by questions outside Europe. . . . Not a single one of the problems outside Europe which had raised difficulties before 1914 caused a serious crisis among the European powers between the wars' (pp. 66–7). I would disagree here and say that it was precisely because of the influence of extra-European questions that the German problem proved so intractable. Taylor admits an 'apparent exception'—the Far East, but adds: 'Great Britain was the only European power on whom it had practical impact'. However, by the 1930s Great Britain and Germany were the dominant powers in Europe and after 1937 the Far East had a considerable influence on British reactions to the European crisis. Admittedly, Great Britain and France did not go to war over Syria but the fierce Franco-British rivalries over interests outside Europe embittered their general relations and hindered the prospects of agreement on European matters. One final point: in the 1930s France became increasingly preoccupied with her empire and Mediterranean position. The result was that when Germany challenged the peace settlement in central Europe from 1936 to 1939 France gave first consideration to the defence of her North African and Mediterranean interests.

2 Anglo-French policy

The key questions which you must consider are these:

(i) Why did Great Britain and France end up by undertaking in 1939, in adverse conditions, a war which they did not want?

(ii) If Great Britain and France had resisted Germany sooner, could a second European war have been averted?

In order to answer these questions two related themes must be discussed, firstly the state of Anglo-French relations between the two world wars, and secondly the nature of British and French approaches to the German problem in the 1930s.

Exercise 2a

1 What were the causes of Anglo-French disunity in the period 1918–39?
2 Set down the main issues on which Britain and France disagreed. (Taylor and Roberts provide some help but you should also look at Unit 19.)

Exercise 2b

Identify the motives which inspired British foreign policy towards Germany in the 1930s.
(Read *Taylor*, pp. 172–4; *Roberts*, pp. 398, 491, 508–9.)

Figure 2   Haile Selassie, King of Ethiopia, addresses the League of Nations in 1936 (Keystone Press Agency).

Specimen Answers

Exercise 2a

1 (i) A psychological cleavage—the French often regarded the British as too empirical, living from day to day and refusing to make long-term policy decisions. In contrast the French were criticized for pursuing logic blindly in face of reality, for being overfond of constructing systems of ideas and security.

(ii) Long-standing antagonism and rivalry (look at Unit 14, pp. 20–1). In the early 1920s the fact that France was the leading land power in Europe led to talk in Britain of a revival of Napoleonism.

(iii) 'The inevitable differences of interests between a continental state which faced her only likely enemy across a land frontier, and the insular centre of a worldwide empire' (*Roberts*, p. 478). One might add that in the 1920s Britain tended to give priority to imperial interests and continental affairs took second place (see Unit 19, p. 19).

(iv) In the 1930s Britain was increasingly aware of France's internal troubles—social conflict and instability of governments. This produced a certain contempt for France and her leaders.

2 (i) The German problem (including reparations in the 1920s).

(ii) The question of disarmament (see *Taylor*, pp. 102–3).

(iii) France's eastern alliances were a permanent bone of contention, especially the Franco-Soviet pact which France concluded in 1935.

(iv) Divergent approaches to Mussolini's Italy.

In the 1930s, as in the 1920s, both countries pursued different approaches to the German problem. As immediate neighbours of Germany across a land frontier, the French were deeply suspicious of German intentions and continued their search for security. Hitler's announcement in March 1935 of German rearmament brought another blow to the peace treaties and led the French to intensify their efforts to secure allies against Germany. In May 1935 France concluded with the Soviet Union a pact of non-aggression and mutual assistance. In June of the same year France and Italy agreed on measures of military co-operation in the event of a German move against Austria. In contrast, Britain was trying to reach an understanding with Germany through bilateral agreement. By the Anglo-German Naval Agreement of June 1935 Britain accepted German naval rearmament provided it was limited to thirty-five per cent of British tonnage. Britain and France told each other next to nothing about their respective negotiations. Italo-French friendship which had been built up in 1934–1935 was shattered by Mussolini's attack on Ethiopia in October 1935. The Ethiopian conflict created new tensions between Britain and France. Britain's adoption of sanctions against Italy received only lukewarm support from France. The British felt the French were betraying the League and collective security. The French were desperately trying to keep Italian friendship as a makeweight against Germany. The Ethiopian affair led to a complete estrangement between France and Italy. By contrast, from 1937 onwards, the British government under Neville Chamberlain made persistent efforts to win Italian friendship. As regards Germany, after Hitler's reoccupation of the Rhineland in March 1936 France reluctantly acquiesced in British leadership, partly because acceptance of British leadership was seen as a means of achieving one of the long-term goals of French policy—closer British involvement in continental affairs, and partly because France could do nothing else, yet the French were still prepared to disagree strongly with her ally. When Germany threatened the independence of Austria in February 1938 France repeatedly asked Britain to join with her in delivering a strong warning to Germany.

Exercise 2b

General considerations influencing British policy

(i) The feeling that the Versailles settlement was both morally and practically questionable—and the belief that Germany had certain legitimate grievances which should be satisfied (*Roberts*, p. 491; *Taylor*, p. 172).

(ii) A general hatred of war and fear that a new war would mean the end of European civilization (*Roberts*, p. 491).

(iii) An exaggerated sense of military and air inferiority (*Roberts*, p. 491).

Neville Chamberlain's personal convictions

(i) Determined to end drift of Baldwin period (*Taylor*, p. 172).

(ii) Resented waste of money involved in expenditure on armaments (ibid, p. 172).

(iii) Believed German discontent had economic causes (ibid, p. 172).

I would add to this list a fourth point: the 'fallacy of rationality'. Both Roberts and Taylor touch on this point without developing it: 'The arms race, he was convinced, sprang from misunderstandings between the Powers, not from deep-seated rivalries or from the sinister design of one Power to dominate the world' (*Taylor*, p. 172); 'His gravest error was to attribute his own kind of rationality to his opponent' (*Roberts*, p. 509). Chamberlain's outlook was grounded in the liberal belief that reason prevails in politics and that most men are basically men of good will. This assumption of rationality blinded him to Hitler's and Mussolini's pursuit of irrational goals.

Conclusion

You are now in a position to explore more fully the two questions with which I opened the discussion.

First let me try to sum up what we have established. As regards Anglo-French relations, the disharmony of the two countries was of enormous importance. As Roberts puts it: 'the essential pre-condition of Hitler's success was the disarray of his potential opponents' (p. 489). Germany's former opponents provided Hitler with a first class opportunity of fulfilling his revisionist aims. Although France tried hard in the 1920s and the 1930s to secure a British alliance, Britain fought shy of committing herself to her neighbour. The treaty of Locarno of 1925 was not the equivalent of an Anglo-French alliance but merely a general treaty of guarantee (*Taylor*, p. 82). Hitler's reoccupation of the Rhineland in March 1936 destroyed the Locarno system and Britain gave France a promise of assistance if she were *directly* attacked, but this was not the start of a real military alliance. Full staff talks were not held until February 1939 (*Taylor*, p. 148). Compare this situation with the pre-1914 period when staff talks were started in 1906.

However, it is arguable, especially in view of post-1945 experience, that a full Anglo-French alliance was not practical in the inter-war years. But, supposing for the sake of argument that such an alliance had been forged, what would have been its impact on events? My own view is that if the alliance had come soon enough (in the 1920s) the German problem might have been contained and controlled, if not checked, though the long-term danger of a European war would have remained. Against this view it might be argued that Germany and the Soviet Union would have joined forces and presented a formidable combination. One might also ask what practical action Britain and France could have taken against Germany if diplomacy failed. Read what Taylor has to say on this subject (p. 103).

Figure 3 Return from Munich: Chamberlain reading the Anglo-German Declaration at Heston (Radio Times Hulton Picture Library).

As regards appeasement, it is clear that a variety of motives were involved, some idealistic, others realistic.[1] The wide popular support which appeasement received up to March 1939 must be borne in mind. Equally important is the decisive personal impetus which Neville Chamberlain gave to the policy. Finally, it must be stressed that the appeasement policies of the late 1930s represented the culmination and development of initiatives taken in the post-1918 decade.[2]

Questions 1 and 2 cannot be discussed without some assessment of the contribution of appeasement to the final outcome of events. How far did appeasement contribute to a warlike situation? According to Taylor, Chamberlain gave 'the first push towards war' (p. 172), and Taylor implies that because Chamberlain provided Hitler with a major opportunity the British leader was as responsible as the German for the outbreak of war. But this is far-fetched. Without Hitler's revisionist ambitions and the will to pursue them Chamberlain would not have devised his 'programme for the pacification of Europe'. More plausible is the argument that appeasement by confirming and encouraging Hitler in his designs indirectly contributed to the growth of a warlike situation. Yet was there a viable alternative to appeasement? You should think about the leadership of British foreign policy in the 1930s. Taylor makes what I feel is a very significant point when he says that Chamberlain was 'driven on by hope, not by fear . . .' (p. 174). In other words, the state of British military preparedness was not the most important consideration in Chamberlain's outlook. Note also what Roberts has to say about Chamberlain (p. 398).

[1] The best intellectual analysis and defence of appeasement came from an eminent historian, E. H. Carr, in *The Twenty Years' Crisis, 1919–1939*, Macmillan, 1939.

[2] Martin Gilbert's *The Roots of Appeasement*, Weidenfeld and Nicolson, 1966 is valuable in this respect.

*Figure 4   Unemployed
man with a poster reading
'I am looking for work
of any kind' in a Berlin
Street, 1930 (Staatssbiblio-
thek Berlin. Preussicher
Kulturbesitz Bildarchiv.
Photo: Herbert Hoffman).*

3   Effects of the Great Depression

With the world economic crisis we come to the great divide of the inter-war years.
One of the questions which you examined in Unit 19 was the causation of the
depression, in particular the relationship between the First World War and the
depression. The question is to some extent unanswerable and a recent study of
the British economy between the wars concludes that 'the war was a secondary
factor in determining economic development between 1918 and 1939.'[1] However,
the aspect of the depression which concerns us here is the evaluation of its effects
on international affairs. In Germany the most striking political effect of the great
crisis of 1929–31 was the emergence of Nazism as a mass political force. From a
small group of twelve elected in 1928 the National Socialists increased their
representation to 107 in the elections of 1930. By the end of 1931 Germany had
six million unemployed.

Exercise 3

The two questions which I would like you to consider are:

1   What effects did the world economic crisis have on international affairs in the
1930s?

2   Given the economic crisis, could peace still have been preserved?

(For this exercise, read *Roberts*, pp. 343, 377, 443–6, 478–9; *Taylor*, pp. 89–90,
152–4.)

[1] B. W. E. Alford, *Depression and Recovery? British Economic Growth 1918–1939*, Macmillan,
1972, p. 81.

Specimen Answers

1   (i) Growth of economic nationalism leading to 'policies of withdrawal and isolation' (*Roberts*, p. 343).

(ii) Goodwill which had sustained international co-operation evaporates (*Roberts*, p. 479). Germany stops payment of foreign debts and economic crisis settles reparations question. 'American isolationism strengthened by the spectacle of former Allies welshing on their creditors' (*Roberts*, p. 479).

(iii) Economic crisis revives and strengthens German nationalism and grievances against Versailles settlement (*Taylor*, pp. 89–90).

(iv) Depression leads to a turning away from international affairs (*Taylor*, p. 89).

(v) Psychological effects of the great crisis continued to inspire British foreign policy throughout the 1930s, 'the confidence of the City of London came first; armaments second' (*Taylor*, p. 154).

2   We can begin to answer this question by asking whether there was a direct relationship between the great crisis of 1929–31 and the outbreak of war in 1939. The suggested economic explanations of the war will be examined separately but two points are worth making in this context. Firstly, by the late 1930s, with the exception of France, the world economy was moving out of the depression and in Germany there was full employment. Secondly, in the unfolding of the crises which immediately preceded the outbreak of war, one is struck by the primacy of political motives, and economic considerations seem to have played only a secondary role in the causation of the conflict. Yet there is no doubt that the world economic crisis profoundly influenced the climate of international relations after 1929. The preoccupation with domestic problems which came with the depression allowed foreign dangers to grow unchecked. It might be argued that the depression was more important as a determining cause of World War II than either the German problem or the peace treaties. As you saw in Unit 19 the prospects for peace at the end of the 1920s were relatively promising and much seemed to have been achieved. Conceivably the problems of German revisionism and nationalism might have been peacefully controlled but for the fact that the whole context of international affairs was changed and distorted by the economic convulsions of 1929–31. The depression placed an additional strain on the fragile international system. In Britain and France the crisis fostered a mood of pessimism and national self-doubt and, as Taylor remarks, the governments of the two countries were more concerned to balance their budgets than to spend, as it seemed to them, wastefully on rearmament. Given the liberal free-trade principles of the period the appeasement of Hitler was to some extent an economic necessity. All this is not to say that a European war was inevitable. The climate of international relations was changed for the worse and the preservation of peace became much more difficult but the actual course of international affairs was determined primarily by the diplomatic moves of the European great powers from 1933 to 1939.

4   Hitler and National Socialism

The argument so far has been to show that there were certain distinctive features (political, economic and social) of the post-1918 international scene which made it probable that a second European war would occur. However, the question to which you must give close consideration is why did war break out in 1939. Much of the answer to this question turns on an assessment of Hitler and his ideology of Nazism. Two themes in particular require attention; in the first place were Hitler's aims warlike and, if so, what kind of a war did he envisage, and in the second (here I am taking up a theme which Dr Tim Mason stresses in the radio programme), was there a 'powerful expansionist dynamic' at work in Germany in the late 1930s, of which National Socialism was a major component?

Exercise 4

1 Indicate briefly Taylor's and Roberts's opinions of Hitler's contribution to events, 1936–9.

2 What is Taylor's view of Hitler's personality?

Specimen Answers

1 Roberts has the following points:

'His demands did not seem very unusual; their danger lay in a limitlessness which was not apparent' (p. 492).

'His decisive contribution to German diplomacy was . . . not one of content, but of technique' (p. 492).

'From 1937 to 1941 . . . European history is, in the main, the story of German initiative, aggrandizement and triumph' (p. 504).

Taylor has the following:

'He aimed to make Germany the dominant Power in Europe and maybe, more remotely, in the world' (p. 27).

'Hitler did not make plans—for world conquest or for anything else. He assumed that others would provide opportunities, and that he would seize them' (p. 172).

'He remained passive according to his usual method; accepting offers from others, not making demands himself' (p. 175).

'The war of 1939, far from being premeditated, was a mistake, the result on both sides of diplomatic blunders' (p. 269).

2 'Many however believe that Hitler was a modern Attila, loving destruction for its own sake and therefore bent on war. . . . There is no arguing with such dogmas. Hitler was an extraordinary man . . . but his policy is capable of rational explanation. . . .' (p. 265).

Comment

Firstly, it is clear that while Roberts follows the majority of historians in thinking that Germany's initiatives profoundly influenced the international situation after 1936, Taylor strives to show that Hitler did not cause the crises that culminated in war in 1939. Hitler was passive and waited for others to offer him what he wanted (see *Taylor*, pp. 100–1, where this point is also stressed). A number of criticisms might be made of Taylor's explanation of Hitler's policy in the approach to war and I will discuss them with you in the final section of this unit.

As regards the picture of Hitler's personality presented in *Origins*, you will have observed that Taylor contrasts two versions of Hitler, what one might call the fanatic and the opportunist, and maintains that Hitler was primarily an opportunist whose 'policy is capable of rational explanation'. Alan Bullock, in his Raleigh Lecture of 1967, takes up this point:

It is a mistake, however, I believe, to treat these two contrasting views as alternatives, for if that is done, then whichever alternative is adopted, a great deal of evidence has to be ignored. The truth is, I submit, that they have to be combined and that Hitler can only be understood if it is realised that he was at once both fanatical *and* cynical; unyielding in his assertion of will-power and cunning in calculation; convinced of his role as a man of destiny and prepared to use all the actor's arts in playing it. To leave out either side, the irrational or the calculating is to fail to grasp the combination which marks Hitler out from all his imitators.[1]

Along with Taylor's exclusion of the fanatical side of Hitler's personality goes his neglect of the ideological framework in which Hitler and his advisers operated. This is the theme which Dr Tim Mason emphasizes in the radio programme and elaborates in his article 'Some Origins of the Second World War'. Of Hitler's beliefs and the movement which he created *Origins* has little to say and this omission constitutes a serious weakness in the general interpretation of the origins of the war.

Figure 5   Hitler and Mussolini at the War Memorial in Berlin (Keystone Press Agency)

[1] 'Hitler and the Origins of the Second World War', in *The Origins of the Second World War*, ed. Esmonde M. Robertson, pp. 192–3.

5   Ideological divisions

The post-1918 world was split by differing ideologies and this ideological conflict provided an additional source of tension and instability. Nationalism was, and arguably remains, the most powerful ideology of the nineteenth and twentieth centuries and, as you saw in Unit 14, pre-1914 Europe was divided by intense national hatreds. Yet left- and right-wing forces presented a new challenge after 1918 because they cut across national political frontiers and their doctrines were world-wide in appeal. The danger of Nazism and Fascism arose from their peculiar combination of ultra-nationalism, political messianism, and totalitarianism. By the 1930s there was no European country without a native Fascist party of some kind and by 1936 a Fascist Europe seemed possible.

Exercise 5a

What effects did Nazism and Fascism have on international relations?

Exercise 5b

What evidence is there of ideological divisions in British and French opinion in the late 1930s?

Specimen Answers

Exercise 5a

'Fascism . . . permanently debased the spirit of international affairs' (*Taylor*, p. 140).

'The statesmen of other countries were baffled by this disregard of accepted standards. . . .' (ibid).

'The non-Fascist statesmen did not escape the contamination of the time' (ibid).

Taylor notes two major effects of Fascism on public morality: firstly statesmen were baffled by the disregard of accepted morality and could think of no alternative but to go on seeking an agreement which would win the Fascist rulers back to good faith; and secondly the unscrupulousness of the dictators rubbed off on to Western statesmen, contaminating their own policies.

My comment is that Taylor's focus is too narrow—by considering only the effects of Fascism on public morality he has missed or avoided the central question of the ideological impact of Nazism and Fascism on international relations. I would suggest that much more was involved than the disregard of accepted morality. Nazism contributed certain irrational elements—*Lebensraum* and racialism—to German foreign policy under Hitler. And Western statesmen mistook a fundamental irrationalism and limitlessness of policy for an unscrupulousness of method and technique, enlisted, as it seemed, for bargaining purposes. Thus, from the point of view of Neville Chamberlain, it was not a matter of winning the Fascist rulers back to good faith but of finding terms which would be acceptable—the assumption being that basically Hitler and Mussolini were at heart reasonable, rational men who would keep their word, provided their main grievances were met. This assumption was not finally shaken until Hitler's occupation of Prague in March 1939. What the Western leaders said in effect was, to borrow a phrase from *Origins*, that once the 'cloud of phrases' (p. 141) which enveloped Fascist policy had been pushed aside there would be a foundation of good will on which a *modus vivendi* might be built. Both the dictators and the Western statesmen moved in the fog of their own beliefs and systems and there was little effective communication between the two sides. Sooner or later a collision was inevitable. Under the title

'The Two Incompatible Worlds' Professor Arnold Toynbee, who himself visited Hitler, describes this mental gap between the dictators and Western statesmen:

An English observer who paid frequent visits to Germany during the span of six and three-quarter years that intervened between Hitler's advent to power in Germany . . . and the outbreak of war . . . had the uncanny impression, as he made the short physical journey . . . that within these narrow limits of space and time, he was travelling between two worlds which were momentarily both in existence side by side, but which could not go on thus co-existing because they were morally so far apart as to be incompatible in the long run.[1]

Exercise 5b

(i) Significance of Spanish civil war for British and French opinion—war 'did much to prevent national unity in Great Britain and France' (*Taylor*, p. 160). It also 'drove a further wedge between Soviet Russia and the Western Powers' (ibid., p. 161).

(ii) Importance of Popular Front in France—'made French unity impossible' (ibid., p. 160).

(iii) Ideological sympathies of conservative circles in Britain and France for dictatorships, though feelings were stronger in France than in this country. Slogan was 'Better Hitler than Leon Blum' (ibid., p. 146). (Leon Blum was the leader of the French Socialist party.)

Left- and right-wing ideologies divided British and French opinion just at the time when national unity was most needed. The divisions of opinion, especially in France, help to explain why no real effort to resist Germany was made before 1939. And these very divisions of opinion contributed to the growth of a warlike situation because they encouraged Hitler to think that Britain and France were too weak to resist him (note, for example, what Hitler has to say about France in Document F5 (Unit 18). One can establish a further connection between the ideological passions of the period and the success of Hitler's foreign policy. What is it? (I am thinking of the way in which the Spanish civil war served to distract attention from Hitler's designs in central and eastern Europe in 1936–8.)

One final comment: the ideological factor made it very difficult for the Western powers to achieve their goals of security and European *détente*. This is a point which Roberts mentions, though you may not have spotted it (p. 489). Until 1935–6 Great Britain and France had relied partly on the League of Nations and collective security; by 1936 the League was dying and new ways had to be found of achieving security. Given the internal dissensions created by the warring creeds, the creation of ideological *blocs* was not a practical proposition. There remained the traditional system of alliances, but Great Britain and France failed to make the most of their own alliance, and alliance with the Soviet Union was not seriously considered until after Hitler's Prague *coup* of 14 March 1939. Hence Neville Chamberlain's persistent attempts from May 1937 onwards to woo Italy. Direct bilateral negotiations with the dictators seemed to offer the only chance to break the diplomatic deadlock. The strengthening of links with France and the pursuit of traditional alliances would, it was argued, only give Germany and Italy the opportunity to say they were being encircled. However, this diplomatic situation played into Hitler's hands. Until March 1939 his success owed much to the fact that he was able to isolate and deal separately with potential opponents.

---

[1] *Survey of International Affairs 1938*, Volume II: *The Crisis Over Czechoslovakia*, ed. R. G. D. Laffan, with an introduction by Arnold J. Toynbee, Oxford University Press, 1951, p. 1.

6   Sociological factors

The 'sociological factors' are to some extent the imponderables in this discussion of the origins of World War II. The 'will to peace' which animated both rulers and ruled in the 1920s and for much of the 1930s helps to explain the vacillation and inconsistency of British and French policies towards Germany. This almost universal desire for peace was probably at its strongest when Hitler was establishing his position in Germany in 1933–5. While a few people may have broached the idea of a preventive war against Germany it was never for one moment practical politics. At the end of the 1920s there was a spate of publications on the war of 1914–18[1] and perhaps it was only in the period 1929–35 that the experience of the war was for the first time fully realized and digested. Allied to this pacifism was a deep dislike for the old pre-1914 balance of power and alliance system, which it was widely believed had brought about the war of 1914. By 1936 British and French opinion was changing. Many still believed in the League and the possibility of general disarmament but did so with an increasing sense of foreboding. Aldous Huxley in *Eyeless in Gaza* (1936) contrasts the idealist Dr Miller with the realist Mark Staithes. Their dialogue was echoed in the debate between realists and idealists in international affairs:

'There', said Dr Miller, 'you're wrong. If one looks for men one finds them. Very decent ones, in a majority of cases. For example, go among a suspicious, badly treated, savage people : go unarmed, with your hands open ... Go with the persistent and obstinate intention of doing them some good ... I don't care how bitter their grievance against white men may be ; in the end ... they'll accept you as a friend...'

To which Mark Staithes replies:

'Huddle together among the cow pats and watch the doctor trying his best anthropological bedside manner on General Goering. There'll be some hearty laughs.'[2]

Nevertheless, the revulsion from war was so strong that a series of German and Italian successes from 1935 onwards was required to bring about the fundamental shift in opinion which manifested itself after Hitler's Prague *coup* on 14 March 1939.

The 'shaking of liberal society' in Western Europe was a very real and painful process. T. S. Eliot's lament in *The Waste Land* (1922) on the decadence of Western civilization is too well known to require emphasis. Society had become 'a heap of broken images'. The powerful national sentiment which had propelled Britain and France into the war of 1914–18 had gone and nothing replaced it. The resulting loss of identity and cohesion left the two Western democracies extremely vulnerable to attacks from the extreme right and extreme left. Hitler's Germany and Mussolini's Italy seemed, particularly in conservative eyes, to be purposeful, dynamic and efficient and this glamorizing of the dictatorships gave the Fascist rulers a considerable psychological advantage in the war of nerves which was waged from 1936–9.

Winston Churchill, for example, was fascinated by the character and accomplishments of Hitler and in 1937 he wrote: 'One may dislike Hitler's system and yet admire his patriotic achievement. If our country were defeated I hope we should find a champion as indomitable to restore our courage and lead us back to our

---

[1] For example: Erich Maria Remarque, *All Quiet on the Western Front* (1929); Robert Graves, *Goodbye to All That* (1929); Edmund Blunden, *Undertones of War* (1928); Pabst's film *Westfront* (1930)—to name only the most important.

[2] A. Huxley, *Eyless in Gaza*, Penguin, 1955, pp. 580, 582.

place among the nations.'[1] In return Hitler and Mussolini regarded the two Western democracies as decadent and weak and this appreciation shaped their policy.

One sign of this breakdown of liberal values was the rejection by many intellectuals of the kind of society which the political leaders were seeking to defend. Capitalism might be in its last phase but there were those who wanted to deliver the *coup de grâce*. In *Keep the Aspidistra Flying* (1936) George Orwell's hero Gordon Comstock observes to his friend and patron Ravelston:

. . . Just look at that fellow's face gaping down at us. You can see our whole civilisation written there. The imbecility, the emptiness, the desolation. You can't look at it without thinking of French letters and machine guns. Do you know that the other day I was actually wishing war would break out? I was longing for it—praying for it, almost.'

[*Ravelston*] 'Of course, the trouble is, you see, that about half the young men in Europe are wishing the same thing.'[2]

Figure 6 Hitler arrives in Vienna, 14 March 1938 (Keystone Press Agency).

Exercise 6a

Indicate briefly how the pacifism of British and French opinion influenced international affairs in the 1930s.

Exercise 6b

Do you think that Taylor would accept Allport's idea of 'Expectancy'?

---

[1] Quoted in Neville Thompson, *The Anti-Appeasers: Conservative Opposition to Appeasement in the 1930s*, Oxford University Press, 1971, p. 59.

[2] Penguin Books, 1970, pp. 91–2.

Figures 7 and 8 Front pages of Paris-soir (*Bibliothèque Nationale*) *and* Daily Herald (*British Museum*).

Specimen Answers

Exercise 6

In the Ethiopian conflict of 1935–6 the British policy of 'All sanctions short of war' (*Taylor*, p. 125) helped to bring about the failure of the League, and Mussolini's conquest of Ethiopia was not resisted. It is true, as Taylor points out, that the so-called Peace Ballot of November 1934 (see Document E2) showed that ten million people in Great Britain favoured economic sanctions, and six million favoured even military sanctions (p. 121). However, the Ballot omitted the crucial question of rearmament to make collective security effective and the timing of the Ballot was important. The crisis did not come to a head until the autumn of 1935.

The pacifist temper of opinion was undoubtedly a factor in British and French acceptance of Hitler's reoccupation of the Rhineland in March 1936 and of the *Anschluss* in March 1938, though on the British side the main consideration was the conviction that on both occasions Germany had a good case for acting as she did.

In the Czechoslovak crisis of 1938 British and French opinion was divided on the issue of German claims against the Czechs and consequently the pacifist current was closer to the surface. A measure of its strength was the enormous relief with which the news of the Munich Agreement of 30 September 1938 was greeted.

Exercise 6b

Taylor does not refer to Allport's theory by name but writes: 'Hitler and Mussolini glorified war and the warlike virtues. They used the threat of war to promote their aims. . . . Germans and Italians applauded their leaders; but war was not popular among them, as it had been in 1914. . . . There was intense gloom in Germany during the Czech crisis of 1938; and only helpless resignation the following year when war broke out' (pp. 136–7).

The excerpt cited above provides an excellent example of the care and caution with which *Origins* has to be read. Note the firm, dogmatic judgement. Public opinion is difficult enough to assess in a democratic society and the Third Reich presents very serious problems of assessment. Before accepting what Taylor says one would want to know the evidence for his assertions.

7   Economic causes

In introducing this topic I referred to the various pre-war interpretations. These interpretations are examined in *Origins* and found wanting (pp. 137–40, 266). Taylor concludes: 'Hitler and Mussolini were not driven on by economic motives'. But recent research suggests that Taylor's verdict is too sharp and categorical. While economic motives *alone* may not have played a major role in Hitler's policy, in association with other factors they were of some importance.

Exercise 7a

List Taylor's reasons for rejecting the pre-war interpretations.

Exercise 7b

Comment on Taylor's reasons. This second question may seem difficult and if you are at a loss then go straight on to the specimen answers.

Specimen Answers
Exercise 7a

(i) Capitalism inevitably leading to war: a 'general explanation which explained everything and nothing'; 'Before 1939, the great capitalist states were the most anxious to avoid war.'

(ii) Fascism's momentum could only be sustained by war: the German economy under Hitler depended more on public works expenditure than on armaments; even if the economy had relied on armaments there was no over-production of arms since several years were needed before full rearmament was completed.

(iii) Inadequate access to foreign markets and supplies: Germany not short of markets—she had monopoly of trade with south-eastern Europe; no shortage of raw materials in World War II; Germany not over-populated; Hitler never responded to offers of economic and colonial concessions.

Exercise 7b

(i) What Taylor says here seems quite convincing. However, as regards (ii) and (iii) his argument is less than convincing and several historians think that economic considerations were an important element in German foreign policy. Two criticisms might be made about the discussion in *Origins*. Firstly, the analysis of the economic causes is relatively brief and generalized. Secondly, Taylor's discussion does not take account of the complex interplay between economic, political, military and ideological factors. It is interesting to compare Taylor's views with those of Dr Tim Mason who writes:

Both crises, the economic and institutional, were acute and insoluble. The Third Reich was the first modern state to face the many new problems raised by permanent full employment, and was totally unfitted to solve them. . . . The economic, social and political tensions within the Reich became steadily more acute after the summer of 1937 . . . the only 'solution' open to this regime of the structural tensions and crises produced by dictatorship and rearmament was more dictatorship and rearmament, then expansion, then war and terror, then plunder and enslavement. The stark, ever-present alternative was collapse and chaos. . . . A war for the plunder of manpower and materials lay square in the dreadful logic of German economic development under National Socialist rule. The sequence of international events was not thereby predetermined, but the range of possibilities was severely circumscribed.[1]

Alas, one must close on an inconclusive note. The debate continues. There is no consensus among historians about the state of the German economy in the years 1933 to 1939. A recent survey of the subject, while not accepting Dr Mason's argument that economic forces were part of a drive towards war, nevertheless shows with a wealth of evidence that 'Hitler was acutely aware of Germany's economic problems, as he saw them, and he was not without an economic theory'.[2] Germany may not have been over-populated and may have had adequate supplies of raw materials but Hitler's analysis, as he understood it, of Germany's economic situation in the late 1930s led him to conclude that Germany could never achieve 'world power' with her own economic resources—she must expand them through conquest. The belief in *Lebensraum* may not have made much sense—economically or politically—but it drove Hitler forward to conquer Russia in 1941.

8   Extra-European factors

Though the United States and the Soviet Union played some part in European affairs between the two world wars their presence was little more than peripheral. While the United States opted for isolation, the Soviet Union was kept on the sidelines. Undoubtedly the abstention of these two world powers accentuated the imbalance of the international system, making the 'German problem' more acute than it might otherwise have been. If a strong Anglo-French alliance had existed, the absence of the United States and the Soviet Union would not have been so important. Given the lack of such an alliance and the decline of France as a great

---

[1] 'Some origins of the Second World War', in E. M. Robertson (ed.) *Origins of the Second World War*, pp. 123–5; A. J. P. Taylor's reply, 'War Origins Again' is also reprinted in this collection, but the reply is quite brief and does not deal adequately with the points raised by Dr Mason.

[2] B. A. Carroll, *Design for Total War: Arms and Economics in the Third Reich*, The Hague, Humanities Press, 1968, p. 95.

Funk   Ribbentrop Göbbels
" IF THE BRITISH DON'T, MAYBE *WE* WILL "

power, the absence of the two powers was of decisive importance. The role of
Japan was also crucial. Japanese expansion, particularly after the outbreak of the
Sino-Japanese war in July 1937, threatened British and French interests in the
Far East. Chatfield, First Sea Lord and Chief of Naval Staff, wrote on 25 January
1938:

Figure 9 'If the British
don't maybe *we* will',
cartoon by Low, from
Europe since Versailles,
*page 203 (David Low,
and Evening Standard).*

Imperially we are exceedingly weak, if at the present time, and for many years to
come, we had to send a Fleet to the Far East, even in conjunction with the United
States, we should be left so weak in Europe that we should be liable to blackmail or
worse.[1]

It might be argued that without the Japanese danger Britain and France would
have been free to concentrate their energies and resources against the dictators in
Europe. Also, there is the question of Soviet policy. On the eve of the Second
World War Winston Churchill and others called for a grand alliance of Great
Britain, France and the Soviet Union to stop Germany. Such an alliance might
possibly have prevented war.

Exercise 8

1   What was the significance for European affairs of the Manchurian affair,
1931–3?

2   Do you agree that 'Probably nothing could have brought Soviet Russia and the
United States into Europe in time' (*Taylor*, p. 167)?

Specimen Answers

1   (i) 'It diverted attention from Europe just at the moment when European
questions became acute' (*Taylor* p. 92).

(ii) 'It reinforced, with unanswerable arguments, the British preference for conciliation as against security' (ibid., pp. 92–3).

[1] Quoted by Lawrence Pratt in 'The Anglo-American Naval Conversations on the Far East of
January 1938', *International Affairs*, October 1971, p. 758.

(iii) Led to strengthening of League, by giving it coercive powers (ibid., p. 92).

(i) is probably the most important, but on (iii) read Roberts (pp. 480–1) who clearly sees the Manchurian affair as a failure for the League.

2   As far as the United States is concerned, I would agree with Taylor, though his discussion of American policy does not do full justice to its underlying motives. The isolationist urge, it has been suggested, derived essentially from a longing for peace. Moreover, while Britain and France had obvious interests in preserving peace in Europe, no vital American interests were at stake. It was Hitler who by his rather off-hand declaration of war on the United States on 11 December 1941, brought the United States into Europe, turning the European war into a world one. The position of the Soviet Union is more problematical. The publication of Soviet diplomatic papers tends to confirm an existing body of evidence that up to and including the Munich crisis of September 1938 the Russians did want some kind of an alliance with the two Western powers. If Britain and France had not pursued appeasement so vigorously there might have been some chance of an Anglo-Franco-Soviet alliance, though the price demanded by the Russians would have been high. Germany, however, succeeded in bringing the Soviet Union into Europe and the German–Soviet pact of 23 August 1939 gave Hitler the assurance of Soviet neutrality in an attack on Poland. This *rapprochement* of the two powers who had most reason to dislike the peace settlement of the First World War made a second European war virtually unavoidable. Finally, it is worth bearing in mind, as Taylor points out (p. 166), that for various reasons, 'Western statesmen wanted Europe to settle its own affairs', free from outside interference. Given this attitude of mind, the peripheral roles of the United States and the Soviet Union become much more understandable.

Figure 10   Signature of Nazi-Soviet pact, Moscow, 23 August 1939, Left to right: Molotov, Staposikov, a military attache, Ribbentrop, Stalin, Secretary of Soviet Embassy in Berlin (Keystone Press Agency).

20.3 THE MAIN LINES OF INTERNATIONAL HISTORY UP TO THE OUTBREAK OF WAR IN 1939

20.3.1 Before considering what Taylor terms 'the specific events' that led to war in 1939 it is important for you to have a clear idea of the order of events. In looking at the narrative of events in the period 1929–39 two questions must be kept in mind, firstly the central question of this unit, why did a European war break out at all, and secondly, given that war broke out, why did Great Britain become involved in it? In answering both questions the development to which you must give close attention is Germany's winning of the diplomatic and military initiative in Europe after 1935. In answering the second question the topics which deserve close consideration are: Britain's assumption of leadership in the Anglo-French *entente* after 1931, the growth of British commitments to the continental powers from 1936 to 1939. Now read *Roberts*, Chapter XV; *Taylor*, Chapters 4–11 (it sounds a great deal but you have probably read most of Taylor by now); and Section F in your Documents unit (Unit 18).

Exercise

1 In what ways did the Manchurian crisis and the Ethiopian conflict contribute to the growth of international tensions?

2 Would you agree with Taylor that Germany's reoccupation of the Rhineland on 7 March 1936 marked the end of the 'post-war' period? (p. 168).

3 What impact did the Spanish civil war have on the course of international relations?

4 Set down the timetable of major events from the Rhineland *coup* of 7 March 1936 to the outbreak of the Second World War on 3 September 1939.

5 By what stages did Britain become involved in continental commitments and in what ways did these stages relate to the developments outlined in question 4?

Specimen Answers

1 For the significance of the Manchurian crisis see my discussion of the extra-European factors.

The Ethiopian conflict: threat of a Mediterranean conflict destroys 'Stresa front' of Britain, France and Italy, formed at Stresa conference in April 1935; distracts attention from German designs in central Europe; creates mistrust between Britain and France; destroys Franco-Italian friendship; gives death blow to the League of Nations and concept of collective security; helps to bring Germany and Italy together in Rome-Berlin Axis.

2 Germany's reoccupation of the demilitarized Rhineland on 7 March 1936 was Hitler's first major success. As well as removing a central pillar of the Versailles peace settlement, the reoccupation destroyed the Locarno guarantees which had given France a semblance of security since 1925. The Rhineland marked the beginning of three years of mounting tension in Europe. Germany started to fortify the Rhineland frontier with France and the success of the Rhineland move encouraged Hitler to think of further moves against Austria and Czechoslovakia. After 7 March 1936 people began to think seriously of the possibility of another European war. Britain and France took the decision to rearm.

3   Demonstrated the breakdown of international order—although a Non-Intervention committee was set up on British initiative and all the powers were represented, Germany, Italy and the Soviet Union continued to send arms and men to Spain; revived the danger of a Mediterranean war between Britain and France on the one side, and Italy and Nationalist Spain on the other; like the Ethiopian conflict, the Spanish war gave Germany useful cover for her ambitions in central Europe; the ideological issues of the war undermined national unity in Britain and France; Soviet intervention in Spain sowed mistrust of Soviet intentions; war had a bearing on Czech crisis of 1938—one reason why President Benes of Czechoslovakia surrendered to German demands in September 1938 was because he feared the danger of civil war breaking out in Czechoslovakia, thus affording Germany a pretext for intervention; psychological effects of the war were important because they tended to break down resistance to the idea of another war—Spanish war created the feeling that Europe was already on the brink of a general conflict.

Figure 11   Czech woman giving Nazi salute on entry of German troops into Czechoslovakia, 1 October 1938 (Keystone Press Agency).

4   *7 March 1936*   Hitler's reoccupation of the Rhineland.

18 July 1936   Outbreak of the Spanish civil war.

24 October 1936   'October Protocols' between Germany and Italy.

1 November 1936   Mussolini announced formation of a Rome–Berlin Axis.

26 November 1936   Anti-Comintern Pact between Germany and Japan (Italy adheres a year later).

29 May 1937   Neville Chamberlain succeeds Stanley Baldwin as Prime Minister.

July 1937   Japanese begin advance into China.

5 November 1937   Hitler's conference with advisers.

19 November 1937   Lord Halifax visits Hitler.

Figure 12 Lord Halifax visits Goering, 26 November 1937, at Carintaall (Staatsbibliothek Berlin. Preussicher Kulturbesitz Bildarchiv).

12 March 1938	The *Anschluss* with Austria.
30 May 1938	In secret directive Hitler decides to 'smash Czechoslovakia by military action in the near future'.
12 September 1938	Hitler's speech at Nuremberg demanding self-determination for Sudeten German minority in Czechoslovakia.
15 September 1938	Chamberlain meets Hitler at Berchtesgaden.
22–3 September 1938	Chamberlain–Hitler meeting at Bad Godesberg.
28 September 1938	British Fleet mobilized.
29–30 September 1938	Conference at Munich of Britain, France, Germany and Italy draws up Munich Agreement providing for German occupation of Sudetenland by 10 October 1938.
14 March 1939	Germany occupies Prague and annexes Bohemia and Moravia.
23 March 1939	Germany annexes Memel.
30 March 1939	Britain gives guarantee to Poland.
3 April 1939	Hitler instructs armed forces to be ready to attack Poland any time after 1 September 1939.
7 April 1939	Mussolini occupies Albania.
13 April 1939	Britain and France give guarantees to Greece and Roumania.
April–August 1939	Britain and France negotiate for an alliance with the Soviet Union.
28 April 1939	Hitler repudiates German–Polish non-aggression pact of 1934 and also Anglo-German Naval Agreement of June 1935.
22 May 1939	Germany and Italy sign a formal alliance, the 'Pact of Steel'.
23 August 1939	German–Soviet Non-Aggression pact. Hitler fixes attack on Poland for 26 August.
25 August 1939	Formal Anglo-Polish alliance signed. Hitler postpones attack on Poland.

31 August 1939	Hitler orders attack to proceed on 1 September.
1 September 1939	Germany invades Poland.
3 September 1939	Britain and France declare war on Germany.

5   After the Rhineland *coup*, Britain gave France a straight promise of assistance in the event of France being *directly* attacked but this was not a full-blooded alliance. No high level staff talks were held until February 1939 and Britain would not extend the commitment to cover France's eastern allies—for example, Czechoslovakia in 1938. However, on 18 September 1938 Britain expressed her readiness to join in a *general European guarantee* for Czechoslovakia (see *Taylor*, pp. 219–20). Taylor makes a bold generalization about the significance of this guarantee but he does not seem to realize, and certainly does not say, that the British government was not offering a British guarantee but merely a readiness to participate in a general guarantee along with other powers. This was similar to what had happened at Locarno in 1925 and did not mean a major British commitment. The real turning point in British policy towards the continent comes after Hitler's Prague *coup* of 14 March 1939. There followed British guarantees to Poland, Greece and Roumania and the attempt to conclude a political and military alliance with the Soviet Union in the summer of 1939.

Until March 1939 Britain continued to conciliate Germany and to steer clear of continental commitments. Hitler's occupation of Prague and the rumours which followed of impending German action against Poland and Roumania brought about a fundamental shift in public opinion in Britain and France, a mood which hardened and grew firmer through the summer of 1939.

20.4   EXERCISES ON DOCUMENTS

20.4.1   1 What conclusions about German responsibility for the war can be drawn from (a) Document F1 (b) Document F5 (c) Document F10 and (d) Document F13? Confine yourself to a paragraph on each document.

Specimen Answers

(a)   This excerpt comes from Chapter 14 of *Mein Kampf*, often called the foreign policy chapter because Hitler concentrated in it his ideas on foreign policy. Two points must be made. Firstly Chapter 14 is only one chapter out of a total of twenty-seven which go to make up the two volumes of the work: the most recent English translation, from which this passage is taken, runs to over 600 pages. Secondly a considerable length of time (fifteen years) separates the writing of *Mein Kampf* in 1924 from the outbreak of the Second World War. In 1924 Hitler was in prison and still nine years away from power. In other words, *Mein Kampf* was a product of German domestic politics in the mid-1920s and the foreign policy chapter must not be given a significance it did not possess at the time.

Contrary to what was later claimed, *Mein Kampf* was not a blueprint for future aggression. However, this does not mean that there is no connection between the book and Hitler's foreign policy in the late 1930s. The importance of this passage and of the work as a whole lies in the revelation of Hitler's basic philosophy which, it is arguable, supplied the spirit of German foreign policy after 1933. If this excerpt is judged in the context of later pronouncements by Hitler one can see a consistency of purpose and outlook. Hitler's basic ideas in this passage are: the doctrine of *Lebensraum*—the struggle for living space in the east, reflecting Hitler's biological view of history as a process of continual struggle; racialism—the superiority of Germans and the inferiority of the Jews; anti-Bolshevism; enmity towards France.

(b)   The document from which these extracts are taken is usually referred to as the 'Hossbach Memorandum' and Taylor devotes considerable attention to it in *Origins* (pp. 168–72). It is, as the title indicates, a record made by a Colonel Hossbach of a meeting of Hitler and his advisers on 5 November 1937. Despite the title of the document, these are not official minutes in a formal sense and we do not have a full and accurate record of what Hitler said. What we have is a copy of a copy, the original and the first copy of which are missing. The memorandum is based on notes written up several days after the conference. After World War II the document was cited in the Nuremberg War Crimes Trials as a timetable for German aggression. In *Origins* Taylor concludes that the 5 November conference had really nothing to do with the formulation of foreign policy—it was an elaborate manoeuvre in domestic affairs against Dr Schacht, Hilter's economic adviser. However, Taylor has since changed his mind and in reply to Dr Tim Mason he writes: 'I was quite wrong in suggesting that the meeting . . . was designed by Hitler as a move against Schacht . . . the meeting had no significance'.[1] But Taylor's conclusion is too negative to carry conviction. There is no need to make exaggerated claims for the importance of the document. Its main importance, like *Mein Kampf*, lies in the revelation of Hitler's mentality and attitude in a general sense. It is also a statement of long-term aims: Hitler wanted Austria and Czechoslovakia— without war if possible, though he was prepared to use force should favourable circumstances arise, and this might happen as early as 1938. Hitler is not planning war in the sense of timetables, but he is thinking aloud and voicing warlike aims.

(c)   The directive from which this extract comes deals with a number of issues which occupied Hitler at this period: relations with recently occupied Czechoslovakia, relations with Britain and France and the Balkan states. This assortment of topics together with the date of the directive, relatively soon after the occupation of Prague on 14 March, provide the pointers to its significance. The key word in the document is 'open' which occurs twice in the extract. Hitler required some time to digest his recent conquests and at this date he is taking stock of the situation, not holding a council of war. The situation is, for Hitler, relatively open-ended. The objectives of policy are clear—a settlement in Germany's favour of both the Danzig and Polish questions—but the methods to achieve these goals are left open and flexible. Hitler is not committed at this date to the use of force against Danzig and Poland but he is willing to consider it. The directive is part of an ongoing policy-making process, and a few days later, on 3 April, Hitler in another directive instructed his armed forces to be ready to attack Poland after 1 September 1939, though this did not mean he had finally committed himself to a solution by force.

(d)   A number of versions of this speech are extant and while all of them basically agree, the version reproduced here is of a much more sensational nature than the others. For example, the detail of Goering's war dance, which might have come

---

[1] 'War Origins Again' in *Origins of the Second World War*, ed. E. M. Robertson, pp. 136–41.

straight from Chaplin's film *The Great Dictator*, is probably a picturesque embellishment. In the other versions Hitler's language is generally much more restrained. The reason for giving you this version was to enable you to form some appreciation of the last pre-war crisis, and especially to bring home to you the fact that it was very much a war of nerves in its final stages in July–August 1939. Hitler spoke to his generals on 22 August 1939; within forty-eight hours of his speech, the British embassy had been given the version which appears here. It seems highly likely that one of the generals present at the meeting passed on this version to the British. But this is almost certainly what Hitler intended. It is arguable that Hitler was speaking partly for effect, endeavouring by a show of firmness to bring off another Munich, a diplomatic solution of the Danzig and Polish problems. And, of course, he was in a strong negotiating position—it was the eve of the signature of the German–Soviet pact.

Exercises

20.4.1   2   Comment briefly on what seem to you the most significant points in Document F6.

3   What are the significant points in Document F3?

Specimen Answers

2   The records of Cabinet discussions are the nearest we can get to top-level policy-making in a formal sense, and both this document and Document F9 will give you something of the flavour of Cabinet meetings. The extract reveals that considerations of military preparedness weighed heavily on the making of British foreign policy in the 1930s, though we do not know whether they were paramount. Another point which emerges is that British foreign policy did not operate in a Eurocentric framework but in a global one. Far East and Imperial interests impinged directly on policy-making and the Cabinet had to plan in terms of possible conflicts in three theatres: Europe, the Mediterranean, and the Far East. Another significant point is the awareness of the policy-makers that Britain is very much on her own; France, her only major ally, is strong defensively but her air force is weak. All these considerations went to the making of a conciliatory policy towards Germany and Italy in the 1930s.

3   The ambassador's report is remarkable for its shrewd and perceptive assessment of Hitler's ideas and régime, especially since the report was written less than three months after Hitler's advent to power on 30 January 1933. Rumbold's analysis of *Mein Kampf* shows that Hitler's early writings had not been forgotten and were known to foreign observers, and this fact should be borne in mind in reading Document F1. It used to be said that if only the statesmen and diplomats of the period had read *Mein Kampf* they would have known what to expect from Hitler. However, as Rumbold's report makes clear, the problem was not to find out what Hitler had said, but to know how far he was prepared to go to put his 'fantastic proposals' into action. Hitler was adept at keeping people guessing and this document is valuable for the way in which it illuminates Hitler's early diplomacy. The cautious and discreet front which Hitler presented abroad was one which he maintained until March 1935 and it was a factor of great importance in conciliating foreign opinion. One final point: Rumbold's report is important because it brings out the extent to which Hitler enjoyed popular support. He represented Germany resurgent.

20.5 THE APPROACH OF WAR, 1938–9

Exercise

20.5.1 Read the following excerpts which are taken from reviews of *Origins* and then answer the two questions:

1 What are the significant points in the reviews?

2 Do you agree with the criticisms of *Origins*?

A ... Here I do not propose to do more than to take one subject, the Czech crisis of 1938, to illustrate the incompatibility of the interpretation which he offers or infers with the available evidence. Taylor's description of the crisis I understood to be as follows: Czechoslovakia was put on the agenda for action by her geographical position and her internal condition; the Sudeten Germans were stirred to 'ungovernable excitement' by the Austrian *Anschluss;* Hitler wished to liberate the Sudetens and hoped that by screwing up the tension something would give; Benes likewise wished to screw up the tension, hoping that Britain and France would thereby be forced to come to the aid of Czechoslovakia; the British brought the tension to a head. ... Hitler therefore could wait with his characteristic patience while the tension mounted and the British did his work for him. ... Munich was thus brought about not by Hitler's planning or pressure, but by British policy ... it was 'a triumph for British policy ... not a triumph for Hitler, who had started with no such clear intention'. ...

Like the rest of the book, this description contains elements of truth and perspicacity, but it is erroneous in detail and wholly false in total impression. It is true that the *Anschluss* gravely weakened Czechoslovakia's strategic position, but this would not have put her on the agenda for action had there not been in Berlin a government determined to destroy her. It is true that differences among the various nationalities in Czechoslovakia were intensified by the administrative methods and outlook of the Czechs and that the Sudeten Germans were encouraged by Hitler's accession to power, but it is not true that the Sudetens built up tension 'without guidance from Hitler' (p. 302), for on 28 March Hitler gave full instructions to the Sudeten leader, Henlein, as Taylor himself notes on page 192. For the 'ungovernable excitement' of the Sudetens Taylor quotes no evidence. ... That Benes also desired to build up the tension is a speculative interpretation which may or not be true, but in fairness Taylor should have mentioned Benes' constitutional and political difficulties in accepting Sudeten demands. ... Finally, it is verbal quibbling to say that Hitler started with 'no such clear intention' as was realised in the Munich agreement: that he had not in the spring of 1938, or at any time, planned in detail the exact course that events were to follow to the *dénouement* at Munich is true enough, but this in no way supports the inference which Taylor draws that he had no plans for the destruction of Czechoslovakia. ... Taylor's fundamental thesis is that ... Hitler did not intend or plan the war of 1939, which was caused, like other wars, by the blunders of himself and others. To sustain this thesis Taylor endeavours to show that each of the crises that marked the road to war—the Rhineland in 1936, the *Anschluss* and Munich in 1938, Prague and Memelland in March 1939, and Poland in August 1939—developed in ways that Hitler did not intend or plan. ...

(P. A. Reynolds, 'Hitler's War', in *History*, October 1961, pp. 212–7.)

B ... it is necessary to uncover two other errors in logic which are closely related and which enter directly into his treatment of those events. Just as his interpretation of the crises that began in 1936 is central to the doubt he casts, at the beginning of the book, on the almost universal view that Hitler 'planned the Second World War', that 'his will alone caused it', so it is central to his analysis of these crises that in no case was German policy the cause of them, All that his evidence can be strained to yield, on the most generous of conditions, is that German *planning* did not actually *occasion* these crises. He never sees the difference between general policy and precise planning or between cause and occasion. ...

. . . Because of his confusion of plans with policy and of occasion with cause, Mr Taylor's version of the pre-war crises is devoid of all regard for the policy of the man who almost wholly caused them on one level. . . . Mr Taylor's analysis of these crises is insulated not only from all regard for the policy of the man who almost wholly caused them on one level but also . . . from all recollection of the extreme international unbalance that was the chief cause for them on the other. . . . The unbalance was so much the cause of Hitler's policy that anyone else in power in Germany might have had a policy similar to Hitler's at least in its objects. It was so much the cause of war that, while it was practically impossible for other Powers to resist Germany's revisionist attitude up to and including the Munich crisis, and equally impossible that they should not resist it if it were persisted in much beyond that point, it set up the danger that it would be so persisted in. But it does not much advance the cause of historical truth to assert that Hitler was not responsible because somebody else in the same position might have pursued the same course; or to assume that anyone else must have pursued it beyond the Munich crisis, when the risks had become so great and so obvious. What we do know is that Hitler did pursue it beyond that point. And what we can conclude from any objective analysis of the pre-war crises is that it was this fact, not the unbalance itself, that caused the war. . . .

(F. H. Hinsley, *Power and the Pursuit of Peace*, Cambridge University Press, 1963, pp. 328–33.)

Specimen Answers

1   The agreement of both reviewers on the inadequacy of Taylor's interpretation of the pre-war crises, 1936–9. Taylor's attempt to show that Hitler was not primarily responsible for these crises does not carry conviction.

After agreeing on this basic flaw in Taylor's book, both reviewers then do battle in their own ways. Reynolds's detailed scrutiny of Taylor's handling of the Czech crisis of 1938 is valuable. Also valuable is Hinsley's alternative interpretation of events, namely the interaction between the international unbalance and Hitler's policy.

2   Since you do not have a detailed knowledge of the available evidence it would be unfair to ask you for a full assessment of the various points made by Reynolds. On the whole I think the balance of opinion would favour Reynolds.

In the case of Hinsley's review you are in a much better position to assess the arguments because the points raised do not presuppose a close knowledge of the sources. The point about Taylor's failure to distinguish between general policy and precise planning is very important. I feel, too, that Hinsley's own interpretation of events is sounder than that offered by Taylor. Hitler exploited the existing international unbalance and, having gained considerable success, refused to modify his policy, thus placing an unbearable pressure on a system which was very close to breakdown.

Conclusion

To round off the whole discussion on war origins I have listed below two major considerations which must be taken into account in looking at German foreign policy in the approach to war.

1   Hitler's personality and policy

Speculation and debate about Hitler's role in events will continue for a long time to come. Two factors have to be borne in mind. First, we have relatively little evidence from Hitler himself: in this period, 1933–9, he kept no diary and wrote few private letters or memoranda. Second, Hitler, like Stalin, conducted a highly personal and idiosyncratic policy, and various influences and pressures impinged on his diplomacy. Well over twenty years ago Professor H. R. Trevor-Roper in *The Last Days of Hitler* pointed out that:

> The structure of German politics and administration, instead of being, as the Nazis claimed, 'pyramidal' and 'monolithic', was in fact a confusion of private empires, private armies, and private intelligence services.[1]

And recent research has tended to emphasize the highly complex interplay of personalities and pressures which characterized policy-making in the Third Reich. One recent writer stresses 'Hitler's constant practice of having a variety of individuals, groups and organisations all working on the same project'.[2] One consequence of Hitler's highly personal diplomacy was the eclipse of the professional diplomats. This decline in the influence of the career diplomats was a general trend of the inter-war years. The causes are complex and do not concern us here but the consequences, I would suggest, did have an important bearing on international affairs. The traditional methods of diplomacy, though slow and formal, were part of the checks and balances of the international system. The trend of the inter-war years towards a much more personal diplomacy of heads of government, by-passing the foreign offices, gave the already creaking international system much less chance to absorb shocks and react to change. The danger of breakdown was much greater when the issue of peace or war hinged on a single meeting between Hitler and Chamberlain.

2   Hitler's military strategy and the state of German armaments in 1939

According to *Origins*, 'the state of German armament in 1939 gives the decisive proof that Hitler was not contemplating general war, and probably not intending war at all' (p. 267). Firstly, what Taylor says here and elsewhere about German armaments must be treated with considerable caution. His conclusions are largely based on a book by Burton H. Klein, *Germany's Economic Preparations for War* which tended to minimize the degree of German rearmament before 1939. Secondly, over the last decade or so, Klein's findings have been reassessed and much more research has been done on this subject of the German economy and armaments. None the less, historians still differ on the issues. You should consult Dr Tim Mason's article 'Some Origins of the Second World War' in *Origins of the Second World War*, and also Esmonde Robertson's introduction. The statistical uncertainties which shroud the German economy in the 1930s make it very difficult to draw any firm, hard conclusions. Finally, coming back to Taylor's statement, Professor Alan S. Milward, the author of the unit which follows, on Germany and World War II, maintains in his book *The German Economy at War* that Germany's pre-war economic and military planning was centred on the *Blitzkrieg* concept of waging short, intensive campaigns intended to bring about speedy victory. Hitler, in other words, did not need to contemplate or plan a general war because he believed he had developed a satisfactory alternative strategy in the *Blitzkrieg* concept. Thus he was armed and prepared for a series of short limited wars, against Czechoslovakia in 1938, against Poland in 1939. It was a strategy which he maintained until the defeats in Russia in 1942–3 forced him to adopt, though very reluctantly, a total war concept.

---

[1] Quoted in Edward N. Peterson, *The Limits of Hitler's Power*, Princeton University Press, 1966 p. 15.

[2] ibid.

The key to understanding Hitler's policy lies, I suggest, in an appreciation of the fact that for Hitler war was genuinely an extension of diplomacy by other means. Britain and France were slow to realize this unpleasant truth. From 1938 onwards Hitler faced Europe with an undeclared war in which all means—diplomatic, economic and military—were deployed to achieve certain political ends. It was a war of nerves in which Hitler, though seeking a peaceful political solution, was in the last resort prepared to use force; and this willingness to use force brought about the war of 1939.

References

Avon, Earl of, *The Eden Memoirs*, 3 vols.: *Full Circle* (1960); *Facing the Dictators* (1962); *The Reckoning* (1965), Cassell.

Bramson, L. and Goethals, G. W. (eds.), *War: Studies from Psychology, Sociology, Anthropology*, Basic Books/Harper & Row (SET BOOK).

Churchill, Sir W. S., *The Second World War*, 6 vols., Cassell, 1948–54.

Klein, B. H., *Germany's Economic Preparations for War*, Oxford University Press, 1959.

Marwick, A., *The Nature of History*, Macmillan, 1971 (A100 SET BOOK).

Mason, T., 'Some Origins of the Second World War' in E. M. Robertson (ed.) *The Origins of the Second World War*, Macmillan, 1971.

Milward, A. S., *The German Economy at War*, Athlone Press, 1965.

Namier, Sir Lewis, *Europe in Decay*, Macmillan, 1950.

Namier, Sir Lewis, *In the Nazi Era*, Macmillan, 1952.

Roberts, J. M., *Europe 1880–1945*, Longman (SET BOOK).

Robertson, E. M. (ed.), *The Origins of the Second World War*, Macmillan (Papermac) 1971.

Shirer, W. L., *The Rise and Fall of the Third Reich*, Secker & Warburg, 1959.

Taylor, A. J. P., *The Origins of the Second World War*, Penguin Books (SET BOOK).

Taylor, A. J. P., 'Origins Again', in E. M. Robertson (ed.) *The Origins of the Second World War*, Macmillan, 1971. ·

Thomson, D., *Europe since Napoleon*, Penguin Books, 1966.

Trevor-Roper, H. R. (ed.), *Hitler's War Directives*, Sidgwick & Jackson, 1964.

Wright, G., *The Ordeal of Total War 1939–45*, Harper & Row (SET BOOK).

ACKNOWLEDGEMENTS

Grateful acknowledgement is made to the following sources for material used in this unit:

TEXT

Cambridge University Press for F. H. Hinsley, *Power and the Pursuit of Peace*; Macmillan & Co. Ltd for Edith Sitwell, 'Dirge for the new sunrise' in *Collected Poems* and for *The Origins of the Second World War*, ed. E. M. Robertson; University of Birmingham School of History for P. A. Reynolds, 'Hitler's War' in *History*, 1961, pp. 212–17.

ILLUSTRATIONS

Beaverbrook Newspapers Ltd for David Low's cartoon from the *Evening Standard*; Bibliothèque Nationale; British Museum; Imperial War Museum; Keystone Press Agency; Radio Times Hulton Picture Library; Staatsbibliothek Berlin. Preussischer Kuturbesitz Bildarchiv.

WAR AND SOCIETY

BLOCK I   The Study of War and Society: Thucydides to the Eighteenth Century
Unit 1   The Historical Study of War and Society
Unit 2   Historical and Social Science Approaches
Unit 3   Thucydides and the Peloponnesian War 431–404 B.C.
Unit 4   The Hundred Years War

BLOCK II   Documents
Unit 5   Collection of Nineteenth and Twentieth-century Documents Part I

BLOCK III   The Revolutionary and Napoleonic Period
Unit 6   The Revolutionary Wars
Unit 7   The Napoleonic Wars
Unit 8   The Conduct of War 1792–1815
Unit 9   War and Economic Growth in Britain 1793–1815

BLOCK IV   War and Society in the Nineteenth Century
Unit 10   War and Technology in the Nineteenth Century
Unit 11   War and Social Adaptation
Unit 12   War and the Idea of Progress
Unit 13   Rudyard Kipling: War and the Imperial Mind

BLOCK V   World War I
Unit 14   Origins and Outline of World War I
Unit 15   Russia and Germany in World War I
Unit 16   The West in World War I
Unit 17   Literature and the First World War

BLOCK VI   Documents
Unit 18   Collection of Nineteenth and Twentieth-century Documents Part II

BLOCK VII   Between Two Wars
Unit 19   The Aftermath of World War I
Unit 20   Origins of World War II

BLOCK VIII   World War II
Unit 21   Germany and World War II
Unit 22   Great Britain and World War II
Unit 23   The Resistance in World War II

BLOCK IX   War, The Arts, and Ideas
Unit 24   War and Education
Unit 25   World War II and the Arts
Unit 26   War and Ideas in the Twentieth Century

BLOCK X   World War II Outside Europe
Unit 27   The Impact of the Second World War on South and South-east Asia
Unit 28   World War II and the Afro-American

BLOCK XI   War, Peace and Religion
Unit 29   The Peace Movement
Uni͟   Religion and Two World Wars

**   II   War in Our Own Day**
         cience and War in the Twentieth Century
         uerrilla Warfare